# Bullets, Booze, and Babes: The Haunted History of Chicago and Illinois

## By Rick Hale

# BeulAithris
## Publishing

Scotland

www.beul-aithris-publishing.com

First Edition

Published 2020

ISBN 9798697264577

Text © Rick Hale
Cover Art © Mark Hetherintgon

No part of this book may be reproduced without the express permission of the author and publisher, apart from fair use in reviews.

# Contents

# Section One: The Haunted Criminal History of Chicagoland

What makes a city? This may seem like a strange question, but it's one that is often pondered. Is it perhaps the tall buildings of steel and glass that pierce the sky? Or, maybe it's the citizens who live, work, and play there. Or, could it be the history of a city that gives it character and it's identity? When you carefully consider these questions the only possible answer could be, all the above. All these things contribute to the greatness of a city. However, when you think of all the good, you must consider the bad as well. Every city, regardless of what country it's in, has a seedy underbelly. Every city has it's muck that threatens to bubble to the surface, threatening to ruin a city's reputation. My hometown of Chicago, Illinois is one of those cities.

From the very beginning of its history, Chicago flirted with the dark side of life. From its humble beginnings as a military outpost on the frontier of a newly born country. To the days when criminal enterprises threatened to tear the city apart with rat-tat-tat of a Tommy gun. Chicago, for all it's good, has always known the bad.

For those that reside outside of our great city, they oftentimes hear nothing but the bad. The negativity that gives sweet home Chicago the unfair reputation of being the murder capital of the country. But, despite all that, we Chicagoans still love our city. Even it's dubious history.

With its violent history and the body count left in its wake, Chicago can lay claim to another famous reputation, the most haunted city in the United States. We have it all folks. We have angry Native American spirits that have been seen in very unlikely places. We have the specters of wiseguys from Chicago's criminal history. We can even boast America's first known serial killer. And we love it all.

Chicago, the windy city, has a lot of history behind it. A history that tells the story of America. I love this town regardless of its history. Criminal or otherwise.

# Chapter 1: Fort Dearborn Massacre

Long before the first skyscraper pierced the blue Midwestern sky. And long before the fire that almost wiped the city from the map, Chicago was nothing more than a field of stinking onions mixed with the vast expanse of the American prairie lands. And the city that would one day boast over 6 million citizens got its start as a lonely military outpost on the edge of the American frontier.

Shortly after the Revolutionary War of Independence, the West was opened up with the promise of a new life far removed from the overcrowded cities of the East Coast. Countless men, women, and children decided to leave the relative safety of what they knew and answered the call of "westward ho." One of the many problems facing these courageous pioneers was the fact that these mysterious, untamed lands beyond the original thirteen colonies were already populated with Native American peoples. And they were not happy about sharing their land with these white interlopers.

As the newly minted Americans moved their families West they were met with various unforeseen hardships. Food and water were scarce promoting many of these pioneers to return to the familiarity of their old lives that they knew to be safe. However, those who continued unabated ran into many of the native tribes that populated these unknown lands. Tensions began to rise between the natives and the settlers prompting the United States government to establish military outposts along the frontier to protect pioneers. Fort Dearborn, in what would one day be Chicago, was one of these forts.

In 1803, Captain John Whistler, along with forty of his best men, built Fort Dearborn not far from the Chicago River. The outpost was large enough to house a full garrison of soldiers, officer quarters, and shelter for travelers who found themselves in trouble. At first, the contact between the military and the local tribes was tense but manageable. Each eyeing the other with caution. There was what could only be described as an unsteady peace between the two.

In 1810, Captain Whistler's command of Fort Dearborn came to an end and Captain Nathan Heald assumed command of the military installation. When Heald took command he did something previously unheard of in military outposts, he allowed the wives and children of his the men under his command to come and live in the fort. Although such a thing was generally frowned upon, Heald argued that such a move could only improve the morale of his men who were lonely at the fort. Having women and children at the fort could only improve the mood.

A few years after the founding of the fort, the United States found itself at war with Great Britain once again. As the War of 1812 progressed the local Potawatomi and Wyandot tribes were all too happy to form an alliance with the British against their common enemy, the Americans. The tribes wanted their land back and this was the only way to do that.

As tensions increased and skirmishes became common, General William Hull ordered Captain Heald to evacuate every man, women, and child from Fort Dearborn to nearby Fort Wayne. Fort Wayne was larger and could be more easily defended if a conflict broke out. Captain Heald convinced himself that evacuating Fort Dearborn was a reckless idea and believed that he could negotiate a peace with the local tribes.

On the morning of August 12, Heald left the safe confines of the fort under his command to begin negotiations with local tribal leaders. The tribal elders arrived as promised but brought along over 500 Potawatomi and Wyandot warriors, something Heald did not expect. Heald met with the tribal leaders and promised to leave behind weapons, ammunition, and all the whiskey they could handle if the tribes allowed the denizens of Fort Dearborn to leave peacefully. Captain Heald, the unlikely diplomat was elated when the tribes agreed to his terms. Unfortunately, those inside the fort didn't share in Heald's joy.

Upon returning to the fort, Heald expected a hero's welcome, what he got was the complete opposite. When he told his senior officers the terms of the conditions his officers chided their leader. Their main concern being, what was stopping the tribes from using the fort's weapons against them as they evacuated. So, Heald did the only thing he could think of, he broke the agreement by throwing every weapon, piece of ammunition, and bottle of whiskey down a deep well. Heald could only hope the natives would never discover what he had done.

The morning of April 16 came and under the protection of Potawatomi guides, Heald and his people moved out. As the party quickly made its way to Fort Wayne, word got to the guides that

Captain Heald broke the conditions of the treaty and double-crossed them. The guides turned on the duplicitous Heald and all hell broke loose.

What occurred on the road to Fort Wayne that day could only be described as a blood bath. The native guides showed no mercy as they viciously attacked the Americans, showing no preferential treatment for women and children. When the conflict was over most of the Americans, and some Native Americans lay dead in the grassy Midwestern prairie.

Today, the Fort Dearborn Massacre as it came to be known, is commemorated by a plaque at the corner of 16th and Prairie Avenues on the near South Side. But a plaque commemorating this horrific even isn't quite enough. Chicagoans had to be reminded of their horrific history more viscerally.

In the 1980s, a mass grave was discovered. At first, researchers believed that these were the remains of people who suffered from an outbreak of Cholera. But upon closer inspection of the bones and finding arrow and hatchet wounds on the bones, it was determined these mysterious remains could only be the victims of the Fort Dearborn Massacre. The remains may have been given a proper Christian burial, the victims of this genocidal rampage are anything but quiet.

Visitors and locals have described hearing screams of anguish and weapons firing in the vicinity of the mass grave. Others have reported witnessing the apparitions of the victims running for their lives before vanishing. People who work and live in the area have reported experiencing hauntings in their apartments and offices. Researchers believe that the blood spilled on that fateful day has forever tainted the city of Chicago for all time.

# Chapter 2: Leopold And Loeb

When you think of murderous criminals, what is your first thought? Maybe you think of a drug-crazed maniac who shoots a clerk while knocking over a liquor store. Or maybe a hardened gang member who kills for revenge. Or, a jealous spouse who discovers their significant other in the arms of a lover and kills them in a crime of passion. These are the first thoughts when murder comes to mind, but remember this is Chicago, forget everything you think you know.

Nathan Leopold, born November 19, 1904, and Richard Loeb, born June 11, 1905, were two men who had everything going for them. Both came from families of immense wealth and power. Both had anything they could possibly want, even great intelligence. It was that superior intelligence that more than likely led these two affluent young men to commit an unthinkable crime.

Following their graduation from college at a young age, Leopold and Loeb were bored and wanted to experience more of what life had to offer. These feelings of anxiety led the two into thrill-seeking, even dangerous activities. But not the base jumping, swimming with the great white sharks thrill-seeking. They needed something they could put their intellect to. Both decided to take up a life of crime.

Over four years, the two friends committed strongarm robberies, vandalism, and even arson to whet their appetite. When they again found themselves bored, Loeb decided it was time to take their criminal impulses to the next level. Loeb convinced his partner that the only way to scratch this itch was to move past their current activities. Loeb told his partner it was time for someone to die. Nathan Leopold didn't even have to think twice.

For several months, Leopold and Loeb hatched what they considered to be the perfect plan for the perfect murder. The two young men believed that due to their wealth and superior intelligence they should be able to pull their brilliant plan off without ever being caught. They could easily outsmart any cop.

After careful consideration of who their victim should be, they chose 14-year-old Bobby Franks, Richard Loeb's cousin. This made Bobby the perfect victim. No one would ever suspect a close family member. With the perfect crime planned, it was time for Leopold and Loeb to put the plan in motion.

In May 1924 when they picked up Bobby, the boy happily got into the car with Leopold and Loeb. After all, Loeb was family, and if you couldn't trust family, who could you trust? Driving a few blocks from Bobby's home, Nathan Leopold brought the car to a stop. Loeb, grabbed his cousin and stuffed a gag in his mouth and smashed the lad's head in with a chisel. Bobby Franks, died a brutal death at the hands of two people he thought he could trust.

When the adrenaline of the murder wore down, Leopold and Loeb grabbed a bite to eat at a local restaurant. Apparently, murdering family members was hungry work. When they returned to the car they decided to double down on the unspeakable act they committed. Wanting to make sure he was dead, they held Bobby's head underwater for ten minutes and then poured acid over his face. They then drove a few more blocks and stuffed the corpse down a storm drain to make sure he would never be found. It was at this point their perfect crime began to fall apart.

Despite all their planning and their faith in their superior intelligence, Leopold and Loeb made two glaring errors that led to their eventual downfall. The first error was, the two self-described criminal masterminds sent a ransom letter to Bobby's parents demanding a large sum of money for his safe return. What they didn't know was, Bobby Franks' body had already been found and identified. This led to the second, and shall we say the stupidest error.

They may have actually gotten away with it if it wasn't for mistake number two - Nathan Leopold had dropped his eyeglasses outside the storm drain where they left the body. It was all too easy for the police to trace the prescription back to Leopold. Both Leopold and Loeb, Chicago's thrill killers, were taken into custody and charged with the murder of young Bobby Franks. And despite what they thought, neither their wealth nor their intelligence could save them.

When the citizens of Chicago learned of this tragic news they were understandably outraged. Despite their immense wealth and social status, the majority of Chicagoans wanted to see these once-promising young men swing by their necks until dead for their heinous crime. There was one man, a local attorney, who didn't share in the sentiments of his fellow citizens. That man was the nation's greatest defense lawyer, Clarence Darrow and he felt that enough blood had been shed in this sad case.

Anytime Darrow was in a courtroom you knew you would be treated to a spectacle. Not only was Darrow known for being a great attorney, but he also had a flair for the dramatic. During the trial, Darrow argued that Nathan Leopold was a dangerous schizophrenic and his accomplice, Richard Loeb was so afraid of his friend he had no choice but go along, otherwise, he would be hurt. Nathan Leopold, despite his affluent upbringing, could not help his murderous impulses, therefore, he didn't deserve to die.

Clarence Darrow was a well-known opponent of the death penalty, believing it to be a barbaric form of punishment. And because of this, he was known to go into great detail concerning what the human body went through during execution. Darrow's flair for drama evidently worked. Although Leopold and Loeb were spared the death penalty, they were, however on September 10, 1924, sentenced to life plus 99 years. In a way, they got off light because the judge that presided over the case was going to send them to the gallows.

While in prison, Loeb was murdered in 1936 by a fellow inmate when Loeb short-changed the man over cigarettes. Leopold's life had a much different outcome from his former partner in crime. Leopold was considered to be a model inmate and due to his outstanding behavior was granted parole in 1958. Seemingly rehabilitated, Leopold moved to Puerto Rico, got married, and wrote a book about his time in prison and was entitled Ninety-Nine Years Plus Life. Nathan Leopold passed away quietly in 1971.

Leopold and Loeb both went to their graves never to be heard from again. However, their attorney and the young boy they brutally murdered are both still very much active. Bobby Franks is buried at Rosehill Cemetery on the Northside on Ravenswood Avenue. Eyewitnesses claimed to have seen the spirit of Bobby playing outside the crypt where he was laid to rest. People have seen him remarked how he was there one second and gone the next.

On the bridge behind the Museum of Science and Industry, the lonely apparition of Clarence Darrow has been encountered. The apparition appears just as Darrow did in life, a grumpy old man in a wrinkly suit and frumpy overcoat. Some have walked past the spirit of Darrow not knowing he is a ghost until they turn around and see him vanish.

Why does the spirit of Clarence Darrow appear on the bridge to this day? Does he feel guilty that the defendants in his most famous case managed to escape their fate at the end of a rope? Highly unlikely, Darrow firmly believed the death penalty was barbaric, and no human agency should have the power to take a life. No one really knows why Darrow remains in this world long after his death. However, if you should happen to cross his path, it's best to give him a nod and move along.

# Chapter 3: The Saint Valentine's Day Massacre

Ah, Valentine's Day, a day when you shower the love of your life with all the flowers, candy, and all the love they can handle. In actuality, it marks the one day of the year when scores of panic-stricken men ransack the card and flower aisle in the store. If you've never seen it, it's quite funny.

February 14, 1929, was presumably no different in terms of the desperation felt in the modern-day. Men scurried about for cards and candy to shower their lady love with. But that particular Valentine's Day in 1929, would be one not remembered for love, but it would be remembered for a bullet-riddled bloodbath. On that day a horrible stain would be left upon the city when the news broke out that seven men were ruthlessly gunned down in the Near North Side SMC Cartage Company.

Leading up to the massacre, the gangs of Chicago were engaged in a war to control the city. On the North Side, George Moran, the boss of the Irish gang was locked in a bitter struggle. Moran was barely holding onto his territory and illegal booze operation to keep it out the hands of the notorious gangster, Al Capone. Capone controlled the South Side gang but wanted the entire city of Chicago to himself. Capone had liquor to sell and a city made thirsty by prohibition was eager to buy it. And Capone would commit any atrocity to make it happen.

As the war raged on, many of Moran's and Capone's men died in the conflict to control Chicago. The local police did their best to control the chaos but they had two things working against them. They were woefully undergunned. And so many cops were on the take, you never really knew who you could trust.

Capone, being the criminal mastermind he was known for being, hatched a brilliant plan that would bring this gangland war to an end in his favor. But would also make his booze the only booze Chicago would ever drink. On February 13, Capone ordered one of his men to place a phone call to Moran, and inform him a shipment of Canadian whiskey was on its way to the city. The caller further told Moran the drop-off point would be the SMC Cartage Company at 2122 North Clark Street the following morning.

The morning of February 14, came and Johnny May, a well-known safecracker was repairing a truck in the garage at SMC Cartage. Standing nearby was his faithful German shepherd, Highball, an ever-vigilant companion. Early that morning six of Moran's guys arrived telling Johnny that a shipment of whiskey was on its way. Johnny was already made aware of the delivery and told the street soldiers to take a seat and cool their heels.

An hour later, all those in SMC Cartage heard a car pull up in front of the building. I'm sure all of Moran's guys thought it was payday. But when they looked outside disappointment gripped. The vehicle that pulled up wasn't delivery of illegal whiskey, but rather a marked police car.

Three uniformed officers and two plainclothes detectives exited the vehicle and rushed in with guns drawn ready to do business. After taking a look around the garage for anyone who might be hiding, the cops lined the seven men up against a back wall.Moran's men were convinced they would all be going to prison that day. Instead, the police opened fire on the seven men. When the smoke cleared, not a single man was left standing, all seven were dead. The only living witness to the slaughter was Highball, and she wouldn't be talking to anyone.

A short time after the killers left, Highball began to bark and howl. The landlady in the next building was annoyed by the dog's incessant barking she called the police. When the police finally arrived, the real police, they were already aware that SMC Cartage Company was an illegal liquor drop off. However, they were not prepared for what they would discover inside. In a backroom, they found the bodies of the seven men laying in an inky red puddle of blood, their bodies riddled with hundreds of bullets. The police knew instinctively this was a gangland hit, but not like any hit they've ever seen. This hit was meant to convey a message and that message was, get out.

When word of the hit reached Moran, the north side boss flew into a violent rage. How dare anyone come on his turf and kill seven of his men. When Moran finally calmed down, he sat in his chair and became thoughtful and simply stated, "Only Capone kills like that." With the murders at SMC Cartage Company, Moran had lost the war to his bitter rival. And where was Capone when the hit went down?

Hundreds of miles away basking in the hot sun of his Florida retreat. Capone was victorious and all of Chicago now belonged to him.

The Saint Valentine's Day Massacre, as it has come to be known as, is a tragic, yet important episode in the criminal history of Chicago. It taught us that violent people walk among us and will do anything to get what they want. The SMC Cartage Company no longer exists, having been torn down decades ago. All that exists in its place is a vacant lot to commemorate a ruthless murder that ended an even more ruthless war. But that vacant lot on North Clark is anything but quiet, as the dead from its violent past still reside there.

Those who walk past the lot have reported numerous strange, even supernatural, occurrences. The spectral forms of men have been seen standing quietly in the lot seemingly unaware of the world around them. The sound of men screaming is carried in the breeze around the lot. Residents in the neighborhood are reluctant to walk past the lot, for fear they may encounter something that is not supposed to exist. And the paranormal activity does not stop there.

When Al Capone, finally went to prison, his fellow inmates would be awakened in the middle of the night by the notorious tough guy screaming in the middle of the night. According to guards and inmates, Capone screams, "Please Jimmy, no." It was believed that Capone was being haunted by one of the men that he had gunned down in Chicago.

Another supernatural occurrence seems to come from the bricks of the wall that bore the scars of the bullet holes on that fateful day. Anyone who has ever owned one of the bricks from the wall the doomed men stood against has met with some kind of misfortune. Owners of the bricks have reported suffering serious illness, divorce, and financial problems. It would appear that these bricks just might be cursed. And whoever owns them may be experiencing what those seven men experienced all those years ago.

# Chapter 4: Adolf Luetgert

As we have already seen with the criminal misadventure of Leopold and Loeb, there is no such thing as the perfect crime. No matter how thorough you think you may be, some minor detail is missed leading you to be caught. No one knows that better than Adolf Luetgert, the real Sausage King of Chicago.

In the late 1800s, German immigrant Adolf Luetgert became a very rich man practically overnight. He discovered that his sausages, an old-world recipe, was a big hit with the people of Chicago. With his sausages in such high demand, Luetgert built a sausage factory and a mansion on the corner of Hermitage and Diversey on the city's near North Side.

Luetgert had it all, wealth, fame and an empire built entirely on sausages. Unfortunately, his empire was incomplete, Adolf Luetgert needed a queen. After a long search, Luetgert met his future wife, Louisa Bicknese, a servant from the Fox River Valley. Luetgert, was so in love with petite young woman, he took her as his bride in 1878. As proof of his love and devotion, Luetgert spent a small fortune on two gold rings one with initials, 'L.L.' engraved on it. The future was looking bright for the sausage king and his lovely young queen, who eventually had four sons together.

As time went by, the neighbors began to notice there was trouble in paradise. At all hours of the day yelling and screaming could be heard coming from the Luetgert residence. The formerly loving marriage was now in a downward spiral into self-destruction. All was not well for the Luetgerts and if matters could not possibly get worse, Louisa discovered her husband was running around in her with Mary Simerling. The marriage of Adolf and Louisa was all but destroyed.

In May of 1897, people in Luetgert's neighborhood noticed that Louisa Luetgert vanished without a trace. Everyone knew their marriage was not a happy one, due to the fighting and infidelity, it wasn't a surprise that Louisa, would just walk away. Adolf's sons approached their father demanding to know where their mother had run off to. Adolf replied she had gone to visit with her sister. His sons believed their father as did the community. Only one person didn't buy Adolph's story, Diedrich Bicknese, Louisa's brother.

Diedrich never believed that his sister just ran off to their sister's home. He knew Luetgert was lying and went to the police and demanded that they investigate his sister's disappearance. The immediately acted by putting one of their best detectives on the case, Captain Hermann Schuettler. Schuettler was a long time veteran of the Chicago Police Department and had a reputation for quickly closing cases. Even if it meant using heavy-handed tactics to gain a confession. If anyone could get to the bottom of Louisa's it was Captain Schuettler.

First, Schuettler questioned some of Luetgert's employees who went on record as saying on May 1, they witnessed Louisa Luetgert storm into the factory. They told Schuettler that they heard Mr. and Mrs. Luetgert yelling at each over money. They then heard Louisa, accuse her husband of cheating on her. They went on to say, that the strange thing was, they never saw Mrs. Luetgert leave. This detail, of course, piqued the interest of the veteran police officer.

As the investigation progressed, Schuettler became more suspicious of the respected businessman. Doing some digging into Luetgert's books, the detective discovered a disturbing purchase made by Luetgert. For some inexplicable reason, Luetgert purchased 378 pounds of crude potash and 50 pounds of arsenic. These odd purchases convinced Schuettler, Adolph Luetgert murdered his wife and boiled her body in acid disposing of the remains. This was all he needed to obtain a search warrant.

When Schuettler and his men raided the sausage factory, they diligently searched every vat and furnace for any human remains. And then the grisly discovery was made by one of the beat cops. Skull fragments and two gold rings with the initials L.L. engraved on it were found in a furnace. Schuettler's suspicions were confirmed and on May 7 Adolph Luetgert was arrested and charged with the murder of his wife. The city of Chicago would never taste another Luetgert sausage again.

When he was put on trial in August 1897, Luetgert maintained his innocence and testified that although he and his wife were having serious marital problems, he did not murder her. The first trial resulted in a hung jury, making Luetgert believe he would be vindicated and allowed to walk away a free man. But, the second trial held in January 1897 had a much different outcome, and the following February,

Luetgert was found guilty and sentenced to one of the harshest correctional facilities in the nation, Statesville prison in nearby Joliet.

When Luetgert died in July 1899, the ghost of his wife, Luisa, was witnessed wandering among the vats and furnaces of the sausage factory. Today, high-end condominiums now stand where the factory was and residents have never reported anything out of the ordinary. However, it is believed that if you're in the neighborhood on May 1, the date of Louisa's death, her spirit is said to wander the neighborhood searching for her beloved rings.

# Chapter 5: Haymarket Square Riot

In 1871, the great Chicago fire destroyed a large part of the city almost wiping it from the map. However, despite the destruction the fire left in its wake, the people of Chicago pulled up their bootstraps and went to work rebuilding their town. They transformed the fire-scarred remains into the metropolis we know and love today.

With the city rebuilt, Chicago experienced wealth and prosperity once again. Unfortunately, unless you were born with a silver spoon in your mouth, the majority of Chicagoans weren't, they never got a taste of that prosperity. Most factory employees, the majority being immigrants, worked long 10-12 hour days, six days a week for very little pay that kept them in the working-class poor. These people worked their tail ends off while men like Marshall Field, George Pullman, and Cyrus McCormack reaped the benefits of these poor immigrants, enjoying everything their privileged lives gave them. And as a result of this, the vast majority of Chicagoans were mad as hell and would do something about it.

Back then there were no laws that protected the American worker and captains of industry took advantage of this. If you got injured or even killed on the job, your family would more than likely go hungry and put out on the street. Because of this, labor and trade unions were formed to protect the American worker. Through these unions, workers demanded a shorter workday, safer working conditions, and most importantly, more pay. Of course, corporate heads did not comply with these demands and they were met with worker strikes and protests. To the worker, it was time to get what they had due to them.

Chicago had been experiencing labor problems for some time and as a result, the tensions between factory owners and workers were raising to a fever pitch. The workers had had enough of their bosses and their refusal to give in to their demands, which were not unreasonable. On May 4, 1886, a mass meeting of workers came together to protest their corporate employers. They also planned to protest the heavy-handed tactics used by the Chicago police when dealing with protesters and strikers. The stage was being set for another fire to erupt.

Labor unions expected 20,000 factory workers to attend a protest featuring such speakers as Albert Parsons, Samuel Fields, and August Spies. These three men were considered socialists and dangerous agitators that whipped workers into frenzies against their bosses. When only 2,500 protesters arrived, the organizers were disappointed but decided to carry on. After all, Mayor Carter Henry Harrison signed off on a parade permit after being assured this would be a peaceful march. The Chicago police didn't share in their mayor's optimism and beefed up their presence to over 600 uniformed officers. They feared that bad things were going to happen.

The labor union proceedings commenced in earnest at 8:30 PM. The police stood at attention in columns just waiting for the first sign of trouble. They knew from other cities that these protests tended to get out of hand thanks to professional agitators. They could feel it coming and were ordered to use any means necessary to maintain order. Mayor Harrison showed up riding his horse and ordered Inspector Bonfield to send a large amount of his men home as he believed this would be a peaceable event. Bonfield refused to send his men home. He feared that emotions were already at a breaking point and didn't want to be left undermanned.

Police Captain, William Ward, will forever be known as the man who lit the fuse of the powder keg. Ward, had had enough listening to these agitators and anarchists and ordered his men to disperse the people, even it if meant them using violence to do so. As Ward's officers carried out his orders, a pipe bomb was thrown into the middle of a 200 man police column. When it exploded one officer was killed instantly and six were severely wounded. The police began firing haphazardly into the crowd not caring who they hit. Someone would pay for that pipe bomb with their life.

Mayor Harrison, from atop his steed, pleaded for calm from his officers and protesters alike. The police completely disregarded the mayor and continued firing on and beating the protesters with their clubs. Hundreds were beaten, arrested, and beaten some more. The identity of the pipe bomb thrower was never discovered, but eight protesters were brought to trial for their participation in the riot. Seven received the maximum sentence of the death penalty and the eighth was sentenced to 15 years of hard labor. Almost a year later, four were hanged, one died in an explosion and the rest had their death sentence commuted to hard labor.

A couple of years after the violent riot, a statue of a police officer was erected at the site of the riot in Haymarket Square. It was to be a silent memorial to the officers who were killed at the riot. Due to multiple instances of vandalism in the 1960s, the statue was moved to the police training academy. Perhaps due to this move, the spirits of the site of the riots have grown restless.

Since the moving of the statue, residents of the area have reported the sounds of disembodied voices shouting and unexplained gunfire. A few have claimed they encountered the apparition of a uniformed police officer standing near the spot where the statue stood. These spirits may be unable to rest because they don't understand that the Haymarket Square riot helped bring about the change the American worker deserved.

# Chapter 6: The Liars Club

For curses to work the intended victim must not only believe in the power of the curse but in the ability of the person who issued the curse. It's psychological warfare at its most primitive. Cursing and hexing is not something that belongs in our modern, technologically advanced age. We are supposed to have evolved past this fear-based superstition. But, the belief in cursed people, places, and things persist, and the Liars club on Chicago's north side just may be one of those truly cursed places.

The Liars Club on Fullerton Avenue, in Chicago's trendy, high-end neighborhood, Lincoln Park is a popular hangout for those that possess a taste for the eclectic. A 'dive bar' as it unabashedly calls itself caters to a wide variety of Chicago's nighttime clientele. Goths, gay and straight, frat boys and everything in between regularly frequent the club. If you're coming here for a quiet drink, or just hanging out with friends, you may find more than just alcohol spirits. Throughout its history, the Liars Club has seen an unusual amount of violent murder and bloodshed, and that stain lingers to this day. This dive bar is cursed by its murderous past.

The first known murder allegedly happened sometime in the 1950s. According to the legend, an abused wife grew tired of being beaten by her violent alcoholic husband. She could no longer take being his punching bag and finally decided to take matters into her own hands. One night as he slept off a bender, she grabbed an ax and buried it deep into his face. Not just once, but several times. When she was taken into custody for the brutal slaying of her spouse, his face was so chopped up the police could barely identify him. Violent murder number one.

Jump ahead a decade to 1962. An elderly man, who was somewhat of a nuisance in the building was beaten to death with a bottle by a neighbor. Reports are a bit sketchy, but apparently, to make sure the job was indeed done, his attacker threw him out the window. Violent death number two.

Lastly, in 1986. Another vicious ax murder much like the first, but this time the roles were reversed. A man could no longer take his wife's verbal abuse grabbed an ax, and as she slept he went to town on her face. Violent, bloody death number three.

Someone might dismissively say, so what, given the long history of the building bad things were bound to happen. While that may be true, you must take into consideration that all of three of these excessively violent crimes happened on the same floor in the same corner. I would say that fact transcends coincidence to the point that something inexplicable may be going on at the Liars Club. And it appears to get weirder at the club because the popular bar is thoroughly haunted.

Throughout its many years of operation, both employees and patrons have reported seeing the apparition of a young woman standing at the bar. According to eyewitnesses, the woman is wearing a dress commonly worn in the 1950s and she just stares at the wall seemingly oblivious to her surroundings. It's believed this ghost may be the abused woman that murdered her husband all those decades ago.

Many patrons have reported the feeling of being touched by unseen hands and a cold wind that travels throughout the bar area. And fairly recently the cursed corner almost claimed a fourth victim. A bar fight had gotten out of hand between two patrons and one of the men tried to cut the neck of his opponent with a broken beer bottle. Even if you're not looking for ghosts, Lincoln Park's Liars Club has a great atmosphere and is just a great place to hang out. I warn you, though, stay away from that corner on the second floor. You wouldn't want it to claim your life.

# Chapter 7: John Wayne Gacy

When you ask any Chicagoan who their favorite hometown celebrity is, you may get several different answers. John Malkovich, an excellent actor with several movies to his credit is one. And if you're a member of Generation X, then you may be more partial to Billy Corgan of the alternative band Smashing Pumpkins. However, we all know who our favored celebrity is, Bozo the Clown.

For decades, Bozo and his sidekick Cookie, owned Chicago TV and entertained generations of children before starting their school day. Every last one of who grew up in the Chicagoland area prayed our name would be chosen so we could try our hand at the grand prize game. Unfortunately, getting tickets for Bozo was damn near impossible and most names, including yours truly, are still on a waiting list somewhere. Looking back, not all Chicago clowns were as innocent or childlike as Bozo. One clown turned out to be a dark, disturbing psychopath who took the lives of many young men in the 1970s. Pogo the Clown, otherwise known as the infamous serial killer, John Wayne Gacy.

Gacy's life started out simple enough. Gacy was known as a quiet child who kept to himself and had very few friends. He was well-liked by his teachers for being very smart and he was liked by adults as he seemed very mature beyond his years. When he was 11-years-old, Gacy suffered an injury that some think may have caused his lack of empathy and disconnection with knowing the difference between right and wrong. While playing near a metal swing set, the swing hit him in the face causing a life-threatening blood clot. After being treated for the blood clot, Gacy experienced blackouts and violent mood swings. These health problems severely altered his personality making him darker and more disturbing than any child should be.

Following graduation from high school, Gacy attended a local business school. After leaving business school, Gacy left his native Chicago and moved to the Illinois state capital, Springfield. It was while living in Springfield that John Wayne Gacy's true nature bubbled to the surface. While he was a prominent member of the local business community and Jaycees, rumors began to circulate that Gacy had a sexual attraction to little boys. In 1968, those unsavory rumors became true when Gacy, was tried and convicted for the crime of sodomy of a minor.

According to his accuser, Gacy tied him up and repeatedly raped him. A psychiatrist testified that after evaluating Gacy, he determined he suffered from an anti-social personality disorder and could not differentiate between right and wrong. When Gacy stood before the judge, he was sentenced to ten years for his deplorable crime. Although Gacy was a menace to society, he did prove to be a model and was released after only serving 18 months. Shocking to say the least. But hey, who says our system of justice isn't broken.

When Gacy returned to Chicago, his mother helped him purchase a home in Norwood, Illinois. Despite his past indiscretions, Gacy was well-liked by the community and he became an integral member of it. He was active in local politics and business, he even went so far as dressing up in his clownish alter ego, Pogo the Clown, to entertain children. This was the days before the internet and nobody was aware that this pillar of the community and entertainer of children was a monster. They would soon discover just how evil he was.

By 1974, the things with Gacy were becoming progressively more bizarre. He started a contracting business called PDM Contractors Inc and would exclusively hire teen boys. When asked, Gacy had an innocent enough sounding reason, he could keep costs down by paying these boys less money. Satisfied with the answer the Chamber of Commerce left him alone.

A turning point came for Gacy in 1975 when his second wife made a disturbing discovery. While looking for some business papers, she found pictures of young boys posed in sexually suggestive positions. When she confronted Gacy with the pictures, he became enraged at his wife telling her he preferred young boys to women. She could no longer take the bizarre man she was married to and walked out.

Although Gacy's wife divorced him, she never gave a reason and no one seemed to care and life went on for John Wayne Gacy. At one of his parties that he frequently had, a psychic came and did tarot card readings for the guests. When Gacy, the respected businessman sat down for his reading, the psychic suddenly became physically ill. Before abruptly leaving the party, the psychic remarked to a couple of people that she saw deep darkness in Gacy. The psychic knew something was seriously wrong with Gacy, but she couldn't quite put her finger on it. She just knew he was dangerous.

A few months after the party, and the psychic's warning, a local boy mysteriously vanished. The police approached Gacy, not as a suspect, but rather because he knew many of the young boys in the community. Gacy, simply said that boys go missing all the time. He may have run away from home. Something about his answer seemed suspicious to the detective assigned to the case. After performing a careful background check, the detective discovered Gacy's heinous crime while he resided in Springfield. John Wayne Gacy, a respected businessman was now considered a suspect. On December 13, 1978, police obtained a search warrant to Gacy's home and made some disturbing discoveries. Gacy had a shoebox filled with the drivers' licenses of young men who had been reported missing. They also found a stash of narcotics, child pornography, and sexual devices. Possessing these items was enough to arrest Gacy but detectives wanted to find these boys. The worst was yet to come.

For months, Gacy's neighbors complained to him of a pungent smell coming from his property, it smelled like something was dead. Gacy told his neighbors he had a mildew problem and they left it at that. However, when police started digging in Gacy's crawlspace they made a horrific discovery and it wasn't mildew. The remains of several missing teen boys were found bound and gagged buried in the crawlspace. John Wayne Gacy was arrested for the nightmarish murder of several missing boys.

Gacy's, trial began in 1980, although only 27 bodies were found in his house, Gacy confessed to many more. He stated that he dumped the bodies in the Des Plaines River and he couldn't remember how many there were at the bottom of the river. John Wayne Gacy was quickly becoming the nation's most prolific serial killer.

When the trial was over, the degenerate serial killer was convicted of 32 counts of first-degree murder and sentenced to death by lethal injection. When his execution came in 1994 and as they pushed the cocktail of life-ending chemicals into his veins, Gacy looked up and his last words were, "Kiss my ass." John Wayne Gacy a horrible person to the bitter end.

Years later, when Gacy's house was torn down, a vacant lot was left where the house of horrors stood. Neighbors reported a few strange things. No grass would grow on the plot of land and that horrible smell of rotting flesh lingered in the air long after all the bodies were removed. Others reported a feeling of dread and feeling physically ill when they stepped on the property. And some people have heard the sounds of a struggle and screams emanating from the vacant lot. Many believed the land itself was cursed and haunted by the young men who met their fates at the hands of a psychopathic deviant.

Since that time, a new house has been constructed and the new owners have never reported anything out of the ordinary. But many residents of Norwood believe that something of its horrifying past remains.

# Chapter 8: Genessee Theater- Waukegan, Illinois

If there is one thing Americans love more than anything, it is to be entertained. We will spend millions of dollars a year to see that blockbuster film everyone is raving about. Or binge-watch our favorite television show on any of the streaming services you can subscribe to. We love to be entertained and always have.

Getting that entertainment fix hasn't always been so easy. Before movies and concerts were so readily available, people had to journey to the nearest city to see a film or hear music. This could not be more true for the people who resided in the small towns that dotted the landscape of northern Illinois. If you wanted entertainment, you either made it yourself, or you watched the crops grow. Boring, I know. That was until three Chicago businessmen saw potential in the small city of Waukegan, Illinois a town 50 miles north of Chicago.

In 1926, A.L. Brumund, H.C. Burnett, and D.T. Webb purchased a plot of land at the corner of Genessee and Clayton Streets in downtown Waukegan. They intended to build a community center that could provide high-quality entertainment at cheap prices and affordable living and commercial space for the people in Waukegan.

Construction of the theater began in 1927 and it was designed by famed Chicago architect, Edward P. Steinberg. The theater was reminiscent of the Spanish Renaissance style to give it that elegant old-world feel. A large dome of hammered silver and terracotta walls made up the auditorium. And to top it off, a luxurious chandelier adorned the ceiling of the lobby. No expense was spared for the people of Waukegan.

For over 60 years, the elegant theater provided a night out for residents of the northern Illinois community. Those halcyon days came to an abrupt end in 1989 when the Genessee theater lost its funding and had to close. The marquee that once burned brightly lighting up downtown Waukegan, was now dull. Thankfully in 2004, the theater received a 23 million dollar donation to renovate the old theater and the Genessee was miraculously resurrected. The theater would once again be a venue for music, plays, and other arts and entertainment. However, there appears to be a bonus to the old theater. The spectral kind.

Since reopening numerous encounters with the paranormal have been reported at the theater. One of those supernatural entities said to inhabit the theater is the spirit of a young girl named, Jeannie. Ushers have reported seeing the little girl playing on the stage as the lights go down. Jeannie also loves to play pranks on the unsuspecting theatergoer. Jeannie, allegedly like to untie people's shoes as they sit watching a show. By all accounts, Jeannie is primarily a happy little specter, but one maintenance man reported hearing Jeannie sobbing and pleading for help. Perhaps life for this little spirit wasn't always pleasant.

If a happy go lucky spirit isn't your thing, and you require a darker, more frightening experience than the first-floor women's bathroom is for you. A large, black menacing shadow has been encountered in or near this bathroom. Whoever is unlucky enough to come across this terrifying specter report that it just seems to radiate dread and fear. No one is certain as to the identity of this ghost, but one thing is certain, it is anything but friendly. No ghost story in or near Chicago would be complete without tales of the city's history of organized crime. Specifically, stories dealing with our most famous criminal, the gangland boss, Al Capone.

Following his takeover of the North Side, Capone and his gang moved the operation further north into Illinois and southern Wisconsin. He discovered that underground tunnels ran beneath Genessee and Clayton Streets and would be perfect for storing and running whiskey. Smuggling liquor wasn't the only criminal enterprise being carried out beneath the theater. Many a snitch and rival met their fate in the basement of the theater. Voices of men pitifully begging for their lives have been heard in the basement. And an apparition called "the hat man" has been seen in the basement. It's believed he was one of the unfortunate men who died in the basement.

The beautiful and ornate Genessee Theater in Waukegan, Illinois is open to the public, offering what it was built for almost a century ago - high-quality entertainment at a reasonable price. Hopefully, it's doors will remain open for many years to come. And hopefully, it's spirits will remain as well.

# Chapter 9: The Snake Lady Of Waukegan

n the 1980s, Waukegan high schools found themselves in a troubling situation. Twelve students of various ages had died from apparent suicides or drug overdoses. Most of the bodies were discovered in nearby Gurney Woods, and according to authorities the bodies were not just haphazardly laying about. They had been arranged in what could only be described as a ritualistic manner. And their hands were tied behind their backs and several were missing body parts. Hands, eyes, and tongues were stolen by some degenerate wandering the streets of their community.

The disturbing revelation caused many to believe a satanic cult may have infiltrated their quiet town. And the suicides and drug overdoses were not unfortunate incidents, but rather something much darker and dangerous. These 12 high school students were sacrificed to the dark spirits of the underworld. Local law enforcement was at a complete loss as to who these dangerous cultists might be. The police may have come short with suspects, but residents knew exactly was to blame. The culprit behind these murders could only be one person, the Snake Lady.

Snake Lady, as she was called, was a local drug dealer who regularly sold hallucinogens and crack cocaine to local addicts. The Snake Lady was also a Satanist and ran a local demon-worshipping cult. It was believed that she, and her followers, sold bad drugs to locals as a means to obtain human sacrifices to open a portal to hell. At first, the police were understandably skeptical of these bizarre stories as they sounded too absurd to be true. They would soon learn otherwise.

After opening an investigation into the Snake Lady, the police discovered where she lived and raided her home. What they discovered would send ripples of revulsion through the police. They found a blood-stained altar in the middle of circle fashioned from bleached human skulls. And atop the altar was a pot with freshly extracted human remains in it. After searching the house, they found the Snake Lady hiding in a closet brandishing a knife. After a fight, the police took her into custody. If she had followers they were nowhere to be found.

While awaiting her trial, the drug dealing Satanist hung herself in her cell. When her body was discovered by Lake County Sheriff's deputies, the Snake Lady's hands were tied behind her back and her right eye and tongue were missing. Although her death was more than a little suspicious, it was still classified a suicide.

Did the Snake Lady really take her own life? Or were other much darker forces at work? Some believe that there was an inside man, possibly a cop who was a clandestine follower, that silenced the Snake Lady. The jail cell where she spent her last few moments is avoided by everyone and no prisoners are ever locked up in it. The sound of a sinister laugh has been heard coming from the cell and terrifying shadow beings have been seen in and around the cell.

I remember hearing about the Snake Lady when I was in high school. I used to regard this story as nothing more than urban legend used to scare local kids straight. However, years later when I was working security I befriended a lake county sheriff's deputy and asked if there was any proof to the story of the Snake Lady. He said to me and I quote, "Rick, it's mostly true." He then walked away with a disturbed look in his eyes.

# Chapter 10: The Strange Case Of Teresita Basa

The very thought of a spirit entity possessing a person and controlling their will is a highly controversial subject in a field of nothing but controversial subjects. Usually, you only hear horror stories of people who are taken over by a hellspawn demon that compels its host to commit all kinds of heinous acts. However, there are plenty of stories in the annals of psychical research that illustrate that spirit possession isn't all bad. In fact, it has even aided the police in putting the bad guys behind bars. One of these cases took place right here in Chicago.

On the morning of February 22, 1977, the staff of Edgewater Hospital learned that one of their own, Teresita Basa, was dead. From what they heard, some unknown assailant broke into her apartment and brutally murdered her, possibly even raped her. Teresita, a respiratory therapist, was known for being a quiet and reserved person. She was also known for truly caring about her patients and always greeted others with a warm smile. No one could possibly understand why anyone would want to harm this kind woman.

Two weeks after the passing of Teresita, the shock of losing a coworker began to fade, and it was back to business as usual. Except for one person, Remy Chua, a respiratory therapist who worked alongside Teresita regularly. One of Remy's co-workers overheard her tell someone that it was terrible that the murderer had yet to be caught. She wished she could just talk to Teresita and help her catch her killer.

After working a long shift, Remy decided to take a nap in the staff sleeping quarters before beginning another shift. An hour after Remy fell asleep, she was suddenly awakened by the strange feeling someone was in the room with her. When her eyes finally focused she was astounded to see Teresita Basa, her dead co-worker staring down at her.

Remy, was about scream when she was interrupted by Teresita saying, "Remy, I want you to call the police.". Terrified by the vision, Remy ran out of the room leaving the hospital.

As the weeks went by, Remy, began having bizarre disturbing dreams concerning the murder of Teresita. She found herself standing in the dead woman's apartment watching her being brutally slain by a shadowy male figure. Not a night would go by without Remy waking her husband with her screams.

One night as the two slept, Remy's husband was awakened by a frightening sight. Remy was sitting straight up in her bed with a vacant look in her eyes. She turned to her husband, and said in the Filipino dialect of Tagalog, "I am Teresita Basa. I want you to call the police." Remy's husband didn't know what to do. He did know that his wife had not lost her mind.

Two weeks after the first incident, Remy woke up again and said, "I am Teresita Basa, you must call the police."

Except for this time she added, "The man who killed me was Allan Showerey."

This time Remy's husband didn't have to think twice, he contacted the Chicago Police Department. Remy's husband knew something inexplicable was happening. When the detectives arrived at the Chua residence and heard the bizarre story they understandably skeptical. Never had they heard such a thing. However, they were forced to rethink their disbelief when Remy and her husband told the detectives details about the case that only they knew.

As the interview progressed, Remy, told the detectives that Allan Showerey, a maintenance man at the hospital was the killer. She explained that Teresita Basa, invited him to her apartment to fix her television. When she went to get something from her room, Showerey, grabbed her by the throat and strangled her until she almost passed out. He then stabbed her repeatedly until she was dead. Showerey then arranged her body in such a way that it looked as if she had been sexually assaulted. To finish things off, he covered her body in a mattress and set it on fire. He left taking her jewelry with him. The police were so shocked by what they heard they left the Chua residence and picked up Allan Showerey for questioning.

While police questioned Showerey, he was helpful. He freely admitted being at Teresita's apartment to fix her TV and pick up concert tickets. But, he did get jittery when he denied killing the woman. He said he could never kill anyone, but the police knew better.

While Showerey was being questioned, his girlfriend came to pick him up. When walked into the police precinct she was stopped by a group of Teresita's cousins. As she walked up to the desk, the cousins noticed that she was wearing Teresita's beloved jewelry. Learning of this, the police arrested Allan Showerey and charged him with the murder of Teresita Basa. Showerey broke down in tears and confessed.

The strange case of Teresita Basa is one of the best-documented cases of spirit possession on record. However, what I theorize is that Remy Chua wasn't possessed. Rather, she was an unwitting spirit medium and the spirit of Teresita Basa could see she had the gift. No one ca say for sure. One thing is certain, Teresita Basa is now at rest.

# Chapter 11: The Congress Plaza Hotel

As a paranormal researcher and investigator, I have always maintained a certain level of skepticism when it comes to haunted hotels, motels or bed, and breakfasts. Anyone can make up a ghost story and in the interest of bringing in customers, they can jack up their prices on a 'haunted room.'

Despite what you may think, it happens and some business owners have no problem engaging in that kind of unethical business practice. While this may be true the majority of the time, many establishments do appear to have legitimate hauntings in their hands. And Chicago's Congress Plaza Hotel in downtown is one of those hotels where the dead walk among the living.

When the 1893 World's Columbian Exhibition came to Chicago, city planners realized they needed a well-appointed hotel to house the more affluent fair attendee. And the elegant Congress Plaza Hotel was built. The Congress as the locals call it, is the city's most luxurious hotel and has played hosts to actors, diplomats, and Chicago's most notorious celebrity, the crown prince of crime, gangster Al Capone.

If you speak to the management of the Congress concerning its ghosts, they will flatly deny that their establishment is home to numerous lost souls. The staff, on the other hand, have a much different story to tell. Housekeepers, bartenders, and even security are well aware of the spirits believed to haunt the hotel. And one of those ghosts is the oddly named, Peg Leg Johnny.

Peg Leg Johnny, is the ghost of a homeless man who was beaten to death on the premises in the early days of the hotel. He got his curious nickname from being an amputee and wearing a peg leg so he could get around. The spirit of Peg Leg Johnny has been witnessed both in the hotel and on the adjacent sidewalk. According to eyewitnesses, the spirit doesn't say much causing some researchers to believe Johnny is nothing more than a psychic imprint. In other words, just unaware energy that has been recorded in the physical environment. There have been several encounters where the witness claims Johnny looks in their general direction, even giving a slight nod of his head.

If you should ever stay at the Congress Plaza Hotel, do yourself a favor and strike up a conversation with the security staff. On the overnight watch, security personnel has reported the unmistakable sounds of a party issuing from the grand ballroom. As they approach the sounds of laughter, music and a ghostly toast complete with clinking glasses are heard. When they open the door, they find nothing. No party, no revelers just a dark, empty, lifeless room.

Not all the ghosts of the Congress Plaza Hotel are spectral partiers or disabled homeless people. The Congress can boast one of the strangest hauntings, I do believe anyone has ever heard of, the enigmatic hand of mystery, as the staff calls it, is nothing more than a gloved hand that sticks out of the walls of the hotel. The gloved hand is believed to have belonged to a construction worker who inexplicably managed to get himself drywalled into the walls of the hotel. There is no historical proof to back up this horrible and unlikely story, leading many to believe it could be just a weird prank. Nevertheless, many people have claimed to see it sticking out of the walls.

The spirits of the Congress Plaza Hotel, appear to be nothing more than residual haunts since they rarely interact with the living. Meaning, they are nothing more than a moment captured in time and replay themselves when conditions are just right. If you should visit hopefully you'll be in the right place, at the right time.

# Chapter 12: Bloody Mary

For generations at practically every slumber party that has ever been held, kids dare each other to stare at a mirror in a darkened room and recite two words three times, 'Bloody Mary'. According to the legend, the apparition of a bloody witch jumps out of the mirror and claws out the eyes of the unfortunate person dared to summon her.

When it comes to stories like this it's hard to separate fact from fiction and fantasy from reality. After all, this all too familiar story has passed into the realm of urban legend. You know, those stories that sound like they could be true but really aren't. However, as far as bloody Mary is concerned there is a sliver of truth this legend. And that sliver of proof can be traced back to the small town of Wadsworth, Illinois, and St. Patrick's Catholic cemetery.

The true story of Bloody Mary's origins did not start with St. Patrick's cemetery, but rather the area of woods around it. Mary, a young newlywed woman, was accused of being a witch by her husband, who was a local minister. You might think accusations of witchcraft died out in the 1600s, but this was northern Illinois in the late 19th century and witchcraft and devil worship was still a part of daily life. The difference between the wrongfully accused women from the early days of our nation's history and Mary was that she really was in league with Lucifer. Fearing she was about to be caught and punished, Mary murdered her husband. Feeling remorseful for killing her husband, Mary went out to the barn that doubled as a dog kennel and hung herself. Years later the house and barn burned to the ground.

As time passed, the Chicago Archdiocese consecrated a small plot of land near the area where Mary carried out her sinister act. And St Patrick's cemetery was opened and began taking burials. Although this was consecrated holy ground, that didn't stop cultists from performing blasphemous rituals in the hopes of raising the spirit of the dead witch, Bloody Mary. Evidence of these rituals have been found in the cemetery and the adjacent woods. Ritual knives and blood stained altars are commonly found as are the bloody remains of animals undoubtedly used as sacrifices. St. Patrick's cemetery seems to represent the perfect storm of dark paranormal phenomena.

Over the years visitors to the cemetery have reported the overwhelming sensation of being watched, chilly breezes on hot summer days, and large black shadows moving among the tombstones. While these experiences may seem frightening, the really bad stuff happens just over the fence in the wooded area.

Before I go any further, I feel compelled to warn you that the owner of the field lives nearby and will prosecute anyone that sets foot on his property. So don't be stupid. Those who have found a way to walk through the woods and field have reported being physically assaulted by a vicious unseen presence. Others have heard anguished cries that don't seem to come from anywhere. Large black shadows have been known to chase people out of the woods. Something does not want people there.

I have visited St. Patrick's cemetery many times over the years and although I've never been chased by sinister shadows, I have felt that eerie sensation of being watched. Something is happening in this small secluded cemetery. Something dark and foreboding.

# Chapter 13: The Grimes Sisters

According to the National Center For Missing and Exploited Children, as of 2015, there were approximately 460,699 children who are missing. Most of these children are teenagers who ran away from home. However, an overwhelmingly large number of these children have been taken against their will, and sadly, will never be seen or heard from again.

Recently, I was having a conversation with a friend on this heartbreaking statistic, and he asked if this has always been a problem. Or, if it's a fairly new phenomenon, that involves children meeting strangers online, who do not have their best intentions at heart. My response was, this is something that has been a continual problem for decades, and thanks to the internet, we are just more aware of it. One of the greatest missing person cases in the history of the nation occurred right here in the city of Chicago in 1956. The case was truly heartbreaking.

As with most teenage girls in the 1950s, sisters Barbara Grimes, 15, and her younger sister, Patricia, 13, were completely infatuated with the dreamy king of rock and roll, Elvis Presley. They listened to his music, swooned to the pictures of him plastered to their walls and now they could see him on the silver screen in his debut film, *Love Me Tender*. And on the night of December 28, 1956, they left their home on Damen Avenue and head to the Brighton Theater, to see their idol for the eleventh and last time.

The girls told their mother, Loretta, they would be home no later than 11:45. She had no reason not to believe them. Patricia and Barbara were both good, responsible girls. When midnight came, Loretta found herself becoming anxious, this was not like them to be running so late without calling. She sent two of her older children to the bus stop at 35th and Hoyne to see if maybe the bus was running late. When three buses came and went without their sisters getting off, they returned home to a worried mother, empty-handed.

Upon the return of her older kids, Loretta called the police stating that two of her daughters went to see a movie and never returned. When the police arrived and spoke with Loretta, they theorized perhaps the two girls had simply run away. Loretta would have none of that nonsense and told the police they were a close-knit family and none of her children would just runoff. The police remained convinced the two girls ran away, but they assured Loretta they would do whatever they could to find her daughters.

As the police opened up a missing persons investigation, their theory that the girls merely ran away seemed to be the correct one. It was reported by various sources they had seen the two girls after they saw the movie. Classmates said they saw the girls at Angelo's Restaurant on Archer avenue 24 hours after their disappearance. A security guard at the Great Lakes Naval Training Center claimed to have given directions to two teen girls matching the sister's descriptions. One source told investigators that they saw them on a bus on Damen Avenue near their home. And lastly, a night clerk at an Englewood neighborhood hotel said the two girls asked for a room but were denied due to their age. Even their idol, Elvis Presley, made an impassioned plea from his home for the girls to return home. When that didn't work, Loretta began to lose hope that she would never see her daughters again. And then hope presented itself.

Almost two weeks after the disappearance, Loretta Grimes received several ransom letters from an unknown person. Whoever the person was, they claimed they kidnapped the girls and was holding them hostage in Milwaukee, Wisconsin. The letters read, that if ever wanted to see her daughters alive again, she should bring $1000 to a downtown Milwaukee church. Finally, she was going to get her daughters back, hopefully, safe and sound.

On January 12, Loretta Grimes escorted by the FBI, traveled to the church the kidnapper instructed her to go to. The kidnapper told her in another letter, that Barbara would walk in and grab the money. If the kidnapper was satisfied with the amount, he would release the girls. Loretta, sat alone in the church for a couple of hours waiting for her daughter to come in. Hope turned to despair when the FBI learned the letters were all a sick twisted joke. A mental patient who was following the story sent the letters to mess with the grieving mother. Loretta Grimes resigned herself to the idea she may never see her girls again. Little did she know her worst fears were about to become a heartbreaking reality.

On the morning of January 22, 1957, a construction worker driving down German Church Road near Willow Springs came upon a weird sight. As he drove he spotted what looked like two discarded retail store mannequins on the side of the road. When he stopped he made a grisly discovery. The two figures weren't mannequins but the naked bodies of two girls. He raced back home to get his wife, and she confirmed his worst fears, they were the bodies of two girls.

When the police arrived, they confirmed that the two dead girls were, in fact, the two missing Damen Avenue sisters. The missing persons case was now a murder case and the police didn't have a single suspect to question. This case was only becoming more difficult. With the investigation into the girl's murders underway, the Cook County Coroner's office performed an autopsy and discovered some interesting details. The pathologist found that due to the girl's stomach content, they more than likely died five hours after their abduction. The pathologist further reported they found no evidence of obvious fatal wounds on either girl's body.

There was no evidence that either was drugged or poisoned. They did find that shortly before death, Barbara, had engaged in sexual intercourse. But there was no evidence it was rape, Barbara had more than likely consented. The coroner's office conclusion was that the girls more than likely died as a result of exposure to low temperatures.

With the coroner's report, the police could begin questioning the shortlist of suspects they came up with. Their first suspect was a 21-year-old drifter named, Bennie Bedwell. Bedwell, bore a passing resemblance to Elvis Presley and may have used that to abduct the girls. Bedwell, confessed to the murders telling investigators that he fed the girls hot dogs and got them drunk so he could have sex with them. When they attempted to fight, Bedwell and a friend, beat them to death. Bedwell's confession was inconsistent with the coroner's report and had to be let go.

The second suspect was a 17-year0old, Max Fleig. Fleig was subjected to a polygraph test and failed it miserably. Fleig confessed to abducting the girls and the police were convinced they had their man. Unfortunately, they had to release Fleig, as it turned out, a 17-year-old was a minor and couldn't take a polygraph test without a parent present. If he was their man, the police lost him forever.

The third and final suspect was a 53-year-old steamfitter named, Walter Kranz. Kranz called police to report that he had seen the girl's bodies in a dream at Santa Fe Park on 81st Street, a mile and a half from the actual site the bodies were discovered. Kranz told police he was a psychic and he knew he could help if given the chance. The police let him go, considering him a harmless nutjob.

As of today, the abduction and murders of Barbara and Patricia Grimes remain unsolved. Loretta Grimes died in 1989, never knowing who was responsible for the deaths of her girls.

Over the years strange activity has been reported where the girl's bodies were discovered over 60 years ago. People have reported the sound of an invisible car screeching to a halt, a door opening and the sound of two bodies hitting the pavement. While others have reported catching a glimpse of two naked bodies laying on the side of German Church Road.

If something unexplained is happening on German Church Road, it would be residual in nature. No one has ever reported interacting with any kind of apparition. The hauntings on German Church Road are nothing more than a tragic incident captured in time.

# Chapter 14: The Haunted Silo

I love urban legends. Those stories that you hear from a friend who heard it from a friend of a friend, but insists the story is true. Usually, the story is fake, even if it does sound somewhat plausible. I guess you could say urban legends are the precursor to 'fake news.' Sociologists, and others who research this uniquely American phenomenon, regard urban legends as modern myths. And just like myths, urban legends typically contain a cautionary tale that imparts a lesson warning the heater not to be stupid.

Sometimes these light-hearted myths take a dark and disturbing turn. The recent story of two girls that stabbed a classmate because Slenderman told them to is a perfect example of this. Chicago and outlying areas are the perfect breeding ground for these bizarre stories. And some may have a kernel of truth to them.

Let's take a trip away from the city and travel to the northwest suburb of Hoffman Estates and the curiously named, Shoe Factory Road. As you drive along, you see an old grain silo among the finely manicured lawns and cookie-cutter homes. Grain silos are nothing special in northern Illinois and generally not given a second thought. But this grain silo is different, because with it comes the burned-out ruins of a farmhouse and a tragic story of betrayal.

Sometime in the 1970s, a farmer, his wife, and their two children lived a modest and quiet life on their farm. Everything appeared to be going well with the family on the surface. However, below the smiles and the seeming innocence, was a much different story. Little did the farmer know, his beloved wife was unhappy with their existence. She had a secret lover she intended to hide for as long as she could.

The farmer supposedly had his suspicions but shrugged them off as an overactive imagination. However, the more time he spent in the community, the more those suspicions were becoming a fact. Stories of his wife running around behind his back were hard to ignore. He had to do something to find out whether or not there was any truth to these stories.

One day, the farmer couldn't take it anymore and devised a plan to test the truth of these stories. If his wife was unfaithful, he would give her the space she needed for him to catch her in the act. The farmer told his wife he was going out of town for a weekend to a farm show. His wife was all too eager to pick his bags and send him on his way.

A few hours after nightfall, when all was quiet, the farmer crept back on to his property and stealthily entered the house. As he walked up the stairs, he could hear his wife in their bedroom laughing and talking with another man. When he threw open the door and saw his wife in the arms of another man, the farmer was overcome with rage. He pulled a gun out of his coat pocket and shot the unfaithful wife and her lover to death.

When the crazed farmer left the house, he set it on fire. As he watched the house burn, he came to his senses and realized his kids were still asleep in the house. A house engulfed in flames. As the burning house fell, the farmer quickly sank into despair and decided he could no longer live. He grabbed some rope and hanged himself from the rafters of the barn. In one night an entire family was wiped out in a fit of passion. Now, we have to ask is there any truth to this story?

According to the locals, there is some truth to this story. And according to the locals, the remains of the farm are very much haunted. The stories of the ghosts of the haunted silo are plentiful. The sounds of children crying have been heard coming from the burned-out remains of the house. And the apparitions of two children have been seen wandering the grounds of the farm. The apparition of the farmer has been encountered as well. Witnesses report seeing the ghost of the farmer making his way to the barn as he drags the rope behind himself sobbing uncontrollably.

The haunted silo is a popular place for local teenagers to hang out. And even if there is no truth to the story of the grief-stricken farmer killing his family and himself, the hauntings appear to be real.

# Chapter 15: Camp Douglas

When the American Civil War erupted in 1861, Chicago played an important role in the training of Union soldiers. In 1861, Camp Douglas, named after Stephen Douglas, the man who lost to Lincoln, was established as a training camp for soldiers on their way to fight the south. Shortly after 1862, the camp changed it's purpose and gained the nickname, "80 acres of hell."

Camp Douglas was converted into a prisoner of war camp for captured Confederate soldiers. When the population of the camp grew, Confederate soldiers began dying from starvation, scurvy, and a devastating smallpox outbreak. It wasn't uncommon to find dead soldiers rotting in their cells from the hot Illinois summers. Camp Douglas, was without a doubt the worst POW camp on both sides of the conflict. The overcrowding of Camp Douglas was a great cause of concern among Chicagoans. At the time, the city was crawling with spies and Confederate sympathizers. They feared these sympathizers would help the prisoners escape and arm them, and also start an insurrection and claim Chicago for the confederacy.

One night, 75 men did escape to freedom by tunneling out underneath the camp. As a result, the Union army brought in the veteran's reserve corp to help with guarding the prisoners. To further make it impossible to escape the camp, sharpshooters were posted around the perimeter with the order to shoot any escapees on sight. Escape attempts became a thing of the past. Prisoners wanted out but weren't willing to do it in a body bag. At the end of the Civil War, when the former confederacy rejoined the union, Camp Douglas was no longer needed. It is believed that over 6000 men perished behind it's stockaded walls from starvation and disease. The 80 acres of hell may be closed, and the nation is one, but try telling that to spirits of the men who suffered there.

Residents of nearby Lake Meadows Condominiums have some fascinating and scary stories to tell about the ghosts of the Confederate soldiers who died at Camp Douglas more than 150 years ago. Screams of pain and anguish have been heard coming from the ground where the camp once stood. The phantom smell of decaying flesh gets so bad at times residents close their windows. Residents have also heard the sounds of soldiers marching in formation and the apparition of a one-armed soldier covered in blood has been encountered on the grounds of the condos. Many a resident has suffered nightmares after witnessing this nerve-wracking entity.

Camp Douglas, 80 acres of hell, has been closed and demolished since 1865. The grounds of this former hell on earth appears to retain the memory of its horrific past as a place of punishment, death and disease.

# Chapter 16: Manteno State Hospital

A couple of years ago, I received a phone call from a friend who had an overwhelming urge to check out one of the most haunted places outside of Chicago. It's a location so unsafe that the police are reluctant to patrol and if they do and find trespassers they will arrest you. Thankfully, my friend decided to stay away from our next haunted hotspot, Manteno State Hospital.

Manteno opened its doors in 1929 after two long years of construction. The hospital intended to offer treatment for people with a serious but not dangerous mental illness. Manteno was considered to be a clean hospital that treated its patients with dignity. That stated mission would soon change. During its first decade of operation, Manteno State Hospital began to grow in size and even took on patients who were considered criminally insane. New buildings were constructed to house the influx of these new and dangerous patients. With the new buildings, new water lines needed to be installed and that's where the fatal error was made.

Patients and staff began presenting with symptoms of Typhoid Fever, a serious bacterial infection that spread quickly and killed indiscriminately. No one could find a reason for this outbreak until some plumbers discovered that the freshwater lines were installed to close to the sewer lines. They fixed the problem, but the disease had already become an epidemic and claimed several lives.

As the disease ran it's deadly course, the hospital came under heavy scrutiny from the state of Illinois. Several allegations of torture and sexual assault had been made against the hospital and its staff, including doctors and nurses. Accusations of bizarre experiments were made by patients against doctors who stated they were only trying to find a reason for insanity. One of these patients who was heavily experimented on was a young girl named Gennie Pilarsky.

Gennie was a girl who suffered from a severe case of manic depression, a mental condition we call bipolar disorder today. Gennie's symptoms and mood swings were so extreme and violent, her parents surrendered their rights and she was placed in Manteno State Hospital for treatment of her illness.

Over four years, Gennie was carted around to different buildings on campus. She was subjected to hours of electroshock therapy, hydrotherapy and as rumor would have it, a botched lobotomy. I can not even imagine the horrific treatment this poor girl had to go through. She was reportedly released and died a very old woman in southern California. No longer able to stand up under the weight of the allegations brought against it, Manteno State Hospital closed down in the 1980s. The buildings began to crumble as nature began to reclaim the property shortly after closing. It hasn't taken patients for over 30 years but it has become a popular destination for local ghost hunters.Visitors to Manteno State Hospital have reported several encounters with the specters of former patients and employees that died from the typhoid fever outbreak. Unexplained voices and screams have been heard coming from the abandoned buildings. One curiosity seeker claimed that a crazed apparition of a woman followed her around the building laughing maniacally and screaming at her. Sinister black shadows have been seen wandering the buildings and the grounds. A few ghost hunters have even claimed being assaulted by the ghosts.

Manteno State Hospital has become a playground for those seeking a good scary thrill. However, I caution you, be careful as the buildings are old and falling down. As far as the ghosts are concerned, you'll have to find that out for yourself.

# Chapter 17: Elfrieda Knaack

Just north of the city, along the shores of Lake Michigan, are several small towns known as Chicago's North Shore. These are the towns where everyone, including teenagers, drives cars far more expensive than yours or mine. And the average asking price of a house is well over a million dollars. The North Shore is where the wealthy elite of Chicago live very comfortable existences.

The town of Lake Bluff, the heart of the North Shore, isn't quite as innocent as some might think. It hides a secret that has oftentimes been called, "Chicago's Great Whodunnit", a mystery that has been at the center of this affluent community for 90 years. And the question that has been on every citizen's lips since 1928, who killed Elfrieda Knaack?

The morning of October 30, 1928, seemed any other morning for the residents of Lake Bluff. An employee of the Lake Bluff City Hall arrived at work to perform a duty he did every single day, lighting the furnace. When he unlocked the door and walked into the furnace, his eyes were met with a nightmarish sight. Propped in a corner of the room was the horribly burned body of a naked woman. Over half of her body was covered with burns that went all the way to the bone. At first, he thought she was dead, but then realized she was breathing no doubt hanging on for dear life. The employee quickly acted and called the fire department.

The young woman was brought into the hospital, where she was identified as 29-year-old Elfrieda Knaack, a Sunday school teacher, and religious book saleswoman. The doctors did everything they could to stabilize her and treat her devastating burns.

When she was questioned by police, Elfrieda answered through labored breathing, "It was my fault. I did it to myself. There is no one to blame."

The doctors and police could hardly believe what this woman was saying. How could anyone do this to themselves? The furnace was too small to fit a body in, and the door was locked from the inside.

Asked about the locked door, Elfrieda, through the excruciating pain answered, "It was locked by a mysterious hand."

Four hours after being brought to the hospital, Elfrieda Knaack succumbed to her injuries and died. Trying to piece together what

Elfrieda Knaack experienced in the basement of Lake Bluff City Hall has plagued local law enforcement for nine decades. Although her death was called a suicide, the police were not convinced. According to Elfrieda, she burned herself to death in a furnace that couldn't possibly fit a body. And this so-called mysterious hand locking the door was absurd. Someone did this to this woman and the police would not stop till they found out who was responsible.

Ninety years later we are just as stumped as the Lake Bluff Police led by Chief Barney Rosenhagen was. We may not know who killed Elfrieda, but a timeline of events was established to try and figure out this murder mystery. And in establishing this timeline, the Lake Bluff Police had one suspect, one of their own.

The day of the murder, Elfrieda had spent the day in downtown Chicago giving a lecture to her colleagues at the publishing company where she worked. She left and bought a round trip ticket to Lake Bluff. The station agent at the Lake Bluff stop told police she arrived around 9:40 PM. A time that seemed doubtful to the police, as it doesn't take over three hours to travel from Chicago to Lake Bluff by train. The station agent would be the last person who saw Elfrieda before being discovered in Lake Bluff city hall basement barely clinging to life.

Chief Barney Rosenhagen was unconvinced this devoutly Christian woman would do such a horrible thing to herself. This suspicion forced him to open a case that challenged the findings of the coroner and cast suspicion upon one of his own officers. Among the evidence discovered at the crime scene were Elfrieda's shoes, wristwatch, and purse found neatly stacked ten feet from the furnace.

If someone was going to kill themselves in the manner Elfrieda allegedly did, why did she neatly stack her belongings? Also noted in the evidence was a bloody handprint on the door, the size of a man's hand. And leading upstairs were footprints of blood and ash. And the most important piece of evidence, Elfrieda had a wound on the back of her head that could only be consistent with someone striking her with a blunt object, a wound that was obviously not self-inflicted. If this was a murder, and it appeared so, why would someone do this to this woman?

Upon questioning a colleague of Elfrieda's, police discovered she may have had a secret lover, a Lake Bluff police officer named, Charles Hitchcock. A former actor, Hitchcock now worked as a night patrolman for the town. During the day, he taught elocution and salesmanship classes in Waukegan. Elfrieda was a student. This was the break the police needed and a possible suspect in the cruel slaying of Elfrieda Knaack.

The police rushed to Hitchcock's house ready to take him into custody for murder. When they arrived they found Hitchcock, his wife, four kids, and the man himself with a debilitating limp. A few months before the murder, Hitchcock broke his leg in an accident, and although it was no longer in a cast, he walked with a painful limp. There was no conceivable way he possessed the necessary mobility to walk up and down stairs or kill anyone for that matter. Police were back to square one.

Ninety years later, the murder of Elfrieda Knaack is still considered to be one of the greatest mysteries in the history of the Chicagoland area. Still officially considered a suicide, anyone familiar with this case knows there is no possible way she could have done this to herself. If Charles Hitchcock, their only suspect, was physically incapable of doing this, then who?

Several people have posited the theory that Chief Barney Rosenhagen, was really the secret lover and Elfrieda's murderer. Two suspicious factors have led people to believe this theory. And I stress, it is only a theory. On the morning after Elfrieda was taken to the hospital, Rosenhagen ordered the janitor to sift through the furnace ashes and throw out anything that was found. And Rosenhagen changed his story concerning the time he locked up the building. If Rosenhagen was the murderer, he was never considered a suspect. He was the Chief of Police and couldn't possibly have murdered someone. Right?

Since the 'suicide' of Elfrieda Knaack, encounters with two ghosts have been reported at the Lake Bluff City Hall that may shed some light on this mystery. In the furnace room where Elfrieda was found, people have heard a disembodied scream, the sounds of a struggle, and the sound of someone running up the stairs. Are these the sounds of Elfrieda being murdered? According to one person, they are.

In the early 2000s, a visiting psychic claims to have made contact with the spirit of Elfrieda. According to the psychic, Elfrieda was attacked in the first floor offices. Her assailant struck her on the back of the head and dragged her to the basement to finish the job by stuffing her into the furnace. The psychic was so overcome by the contact with Elfrieda's spirit, she had to be carried out by an investigator that accompanied her. And as for the second spirit that haunts the building - it's the murderer of course.

The angry spirit of a man in uniform has been encountered throughout the building. When he manifests, he is said to have an angry scowl on his face and yells at people to leave. After seeing the spirit, one witness identified the spirit from a picture. That picture was of Barney Rosenhagen, former Chief of Lake Bluff Police Department. Is the spirit of Chief Barney Rosenhagen, still stalking the halls of the Lake Bluff city hall? If he is it might to see to it the cover-up of the murder of Elfrieda Knaack remains intact.

# Chapter 18: John Dillinger

"Rob from the rich and give to the poor." A noble and timeless philosophy we are all familiar with. This saying comes from the old English folktale of Robin Hood, a fun-loving outlaw who targeted the rich and noble to separate them from their wealth and giving it all to the oppressed peasants. While the historicity of an actual Robin Hood is debatable, the philosophy of helping those in need is not. In the 1930s, the city of Chicago had its version of Robin Hood. But, unlike the hero of old who committed crimes while indulging in shenanigans, John Dillinger, was a cold-blooded killer.

Dillinger, began his life of crime in 1924 when he held up the grocery store in his hometown of Mooresville, Indiana. When the cocky, handsome young man stood before the court, the judge threw the book at him sentencing him to 10-20 years in a state penitentiary. When he was released from prison in 1933 after only serving nine and a half years, you might think Dillinger would live a quiet life while suppressing his criminal impulses. Not likely. When he was released, Dillinger robbed three banks in a matter of three months, netting a cool $40,000, which was a fortune in those days.

Barely out of jail five months, the roguish criminal was captured once again in September of the same year. This time he was sentenced to life and imprisoned in Lima, Ohio. His stay in Lima didn't last long, his gang staged a daring jailbreak and John Dillinger went back to the only vocation he ever knew, robbing banks.

January 1934, Dillinger graduated from just being a bank robber to a stone-cold killer when he shot and killed a police officer in East Chicago. The police caught up with him in Arizona and brought him back to Crown Point, Indiana to await his trial. This time Dillinger would swing for sure. But, fate would have to wait. Dillinger fashioned a fake gun from a bar of soap and blackened it with shoe polish. He escaped yet again. The hangman was denied.

Following a shootout in St. Paul, Minnesota and narrowly escaping the FBI in Mercer, Wisconsin, Dillinger arrived in Chicago. Needing fast cash, the gangster, robbed a bank in South Bend, Indiana where he killed a police officer and 4 civilians that got caught in the crossfire. In just over a year, he robbed 6 banks, gunned down 2 cops, killed 2 FBI agents, and escaped 2 traps. John Dillinger, bank robber, and escape artist appeared to be unstoppable. Following these daring crimes, Dillinger was placed on the FBI's most wanted and considered public enemy number one.

Despite all the bloodshed perpetrated by Dillinger, this menace to society possessed a soft side that was uncharacteristic of the tough guy. This was the time of the Great Depression when millions were out of work and American families were going hungry. Reportedly, Dillinger robbed several banks and gave large portions of the stolen money to those living in poverty. Whether or not this is true is debatable, but the people of Chicago believed it. And despite being a murderer, many of the poverty-stricken citizens considered him an extraordinarily lucky hero. That luck was about to change.

Perhaps Dillinger began to think his luck could only hold out for so long and took drastic measures to remain a free man. In May 1934, Dillinger tracked down a disgraced doctor who lost his license after botching a few plastic surgeries. Doctor Loeser, told the gangster he no longer performed surgeries. However, every man has his price. Dillinger, paid him the princely sum of $5000 to change his recognizable face. Loeser agreed and went about changing the face of the infamous criminal.

When he was done, Dillinger had lost 3 moles, his cleft chin, and the bridge of his nose. When he was all healed up, John Dillinger looked like a new man. He could now walk down the street without fear of some cop arresting him and throwing him in the slammer. Little did he know how wrong he was.

For over 3 weeks, Dillinger was nowhere to be found. There were no reports of daring bank robberies and shoot outs with the local police. Agent Melvin Purvis and his men began to believe, Dillinger, was either dead or had skipped town. Purvis was about to move on when an unlikely source said she knew the whereabouts of John Dillinger. Anna Sage, an Eastern European immigrant had been picked up for prostitution and told police she knew the whereabouts of the famed bank robber. Sage agreed to help Purvis only if he promised she wouldn't be deported. Hungry to take Dillinger down, Purvis agreed to the woman's demands. And the two went over their plan to take down Dillinger.

Twenty-five days after his plastic surgery, John Dillinger attended a showing of *Manhattan Melodrama* at the Biograph Theater on Lincoln Avenue. With him was his girlfriend and Anna Sage. Little did he know that Sage had agreed to betray him by wearing a red dress as a signal to the authorities. Agent Melvin Purvis, along with sixteen police and several FBI agents waited outside the theater for the movie to let out. Soon, was all Purvis could think.

When Dillinger walked out into the warm night air of Chicago's north side a woman on each arm, Purvis confronted the gangster hoping they could end this peacefully. Peaceful was not Dillinger's style and he didn't want his crime spree to end. Dillinger attempted to flee the small army of law enforcement officers by running down the alley next to the Biograph. When he pulled out his pistol to shoot, 4 shots rang out and John Dillinger fell dead in the dark alley. Public enemy number one's crime wave was no more.

After the shootout with Dillinger, the scene at the Biograph Theater descended into chaos. The police failed to establish a secure crime scene in the alley. According to legend, several onlookers dipped handkerchiefs in the pool of Dillinger's blood. They believed this would somehow give them the luck that Dillinger enjoyed. The situation at the hospital where Dillinger was taken to was no different.

Following the shooting, Purvis had Dillinger's body rushed to nearby Alexian Brothers Hospital. By the time they arrived, Dillinger was already dead and the hospital told the agent he needed to take the body to the morgue. When the body was placed in the morgue thousands of Dillinger fans showed up to view the body of their hero. They wanted to make sure it really was him.

Since that fateful night over 80 years ago, people have reported strange activity in the alley where Dillinger was gunned down. The apparition of a man in a blue suit desperately running for his life has been witnessed. Those who have seen the apparition claims that it turns and then falls down and vanishes. Cold breezes even on hot summer days are reported by people cutting down the alley to Halstead Street. I would like to say that what people are seeing is the ghost of John Dillinger living out his last few moments before being shot by Melvin Purvis. But I can't, because the man that died in that alley might not have been the famed bank robber at all.

New evidence has emerged which suggests that it wasn't John Dillinger who died in that alley. The corpse that was brought in the morgue had characteristics, Dillinger didn't have. For example, Dillinger had blue eyes, the corpse had brown. And the corpse was several inches shorter and several pounds heavier than Dillinger. And according to the coroner, the body on the slab had a rheumatic heart condition since childhood. Dillinger's Naval record said his heart was in perfect condition. If this wasn't public enemy number one, then who was it?

Some historians believe the body that was brought in to the morgue was a small-time criminal from Wisconsin, Jimmy Lawrence. It's theorized, Dillinger got wise to the plan to bring him down and paid Lawrence to go in his place. Dillinger knew Purvis would be there. Another theory was that Purvis was in Dillinger's back pocket the whole time, which might explain why shortly after "Dillinger's" capture, Special Agent Melvin Purvis ate a bullet in his home. It's believed that Dillinger escaped to the state of Oregon where he retired to a quiet, crime-free life.

If you should ever visit Dillinger's alley on the side of The Biograph Theater, and attempt to make contact, you may get better results calling the spirit, Jimmy.

# Chapter 19: Emily's Ghost

For many young people, graduating from high school, and going off to college is an important part of the coming of age process. In college, a student doesn't just major in a subject, they also learn about themselves and the world around them. However, the college experience is not always a pleasant one. The ghost of Emily Keseg knows that better than anyone else.

In 1969, 18-year-old Emily Keseg was like most girls her age. She was a freshman at Morton College in Cicero, she had a boyfriend and a group of friends she had known her entire life. By all appearances, Emily's life was right on track. One Friday morning, Emily left for school and did her usual routine believing all was right with the world. The only bump in the road was an argument she had with her boyfriend over a silly ring. After class, Emily met up with her friends and went to a local pizzeria where they met up with a couple of guys from school.

Around 1 AM Emily asked her friend if she would mind dropping her off at her boyfriend's house. All day, Emily felt guilty about the fight she and her boyfriend had earlier that day. The fight was really her fault and she was compelled to apologize. Her friend understood and dropped her off in front of her boyfriend's darkened house. That was the last time anyone would see Emily Keseg alive.

The following morning, a woman on 59th street was awakened from her slumber by a strange noise. She heard what sounded like a person moaning in the alley below her window. When her son returned from his paper route, she asked him to take a check the alley for anything out of the ordinary. A few moments later, he returned with a wig and blood-soaked one-dollar bill. Believing something bad had happened in the alley she notified the police.

Shortly after the police arrived to take her statement, two telephone repairmen discovered Emily's school ID and blood-soaked clothes in the alley. The police officers notified their dispatcher and a search for the girl was underway. A few hours after the search for Emily begun, it ended at 1:30 PM. The naked body of Emily Keseg, was found in a field a block over from where her clothes and ID were found. Her face was bloody and bruised and a huge hole was found in the back of her head. During an autopsy, it was concluded that Emily had been raped several times and strangulation was the cause of death. The community rallied behind the police and a search for Emily's murderers had begun.

Several suspects, including Emily's boyfriend, were brought in for questioning. The boyfriend told detectives that he was asleep until 9 AM and hadn't seen Emily since the day before. Detectives believed the boyfriend and allowed him to leave. The police only had two other suspects in the rape and killing of Emily Keseg, but their alibis were ironclad. To this day the rape and murder of Emily Keseg remain open in the hopes that someone will come forward with information. As for Emily, her spirit is still looking for answers.

Today, Morton College stands in the field where Emily's body was discovered. According to numerous people who attend or work at the college, Emily is still there. Night security guards have encountered the ghost of Emily running down halls and slamming doors in the middle of the night. Students and faculty have seen the girl wandering the halls and the parking lot acting as if she was looking for something. Maybe she is still looking for her killer.

One dramatic encounter happened to a maintenance man on the roof of the school. One day, he was fixing a vent on the roof when he looked up to see a young hippy girl, as he called her, standing too close to the edge. When he approached and tried warning her she was standing to close, the girl jumped. The maintenance man raced to the edge and was stunned when all he saw below were people walking in and out of the building.

Practically everyone who has ever attended or worked at Morton College has a strange story to tell about Emily's ghost. She is even considered an unofficial mascot. The spirit of this poor brutalized girl will more than likely wander the campus until she is satisfied that her killers have been captured.

# Chapter 20: The Tonic Room

In a city with a dozen or more bars all claiming to be the most haunted drinking establishment, it can be difficult to find one that is truly haunted. However, there is a bar on the North Side that not only can claim ghosts associated with Chicago's history of organized crime, it may also be inhabited by powers of a much sinister origin. Welcome to The Tonic Room.

Since the days of the street war between Moran and Capone, the building housing The Tonic Room has had a colorful history. The building was used as a hangout and speakeasy for the North Side Irish gang and the upper floors were a brothel. If you were a young man looking for a good time, the building at 2447 North Halsted street was the place to go.

When the owners of The Tonic Room purchased the building, they could tell they had a real fixer-upper on their hands. It's not that the building was in disrepair because Chicago buildings are built to last. Rather, they needed to make improvements if they were going to convert the space into a bar. But, they weren't prepared for the weirdness they would soon discover in the basement.

As the owners toured the basement, they discovered Egyptian hieroglyphics painted on the ceiling. But, what really chilled them to the bone was what they found painted on the basement floor - a large pentagram. This, of course, frightened the new owners and rightly so. They could only speculate what happened in this basement. They would soon find out the disturbing occult history of the building.

When the owners conducted some historical research, they discovered the basement may have been used as a meeting place for an occult secret society called The Golden Dawn. The further they dug into the building's past, the more disturbing it became. According to a local woman, when she was a child in the 1930s, her father took her to a secret meeting in the basement. She claimed to have witnessed a ritual sacrifice, and the occult practices didn't stop there.

In 1969, the building was a boutique called, El-Sabarum, and it catered to people with an interest in the occult and the supernatural. You could everything from magical amulets, various herbs even Voodoo beads. The owner of the boutique, Frederic De'Arechaga, considered himself to be the 'Pontifus Maximus' of a Sabaen religious order. Sabaean was a pre-Islamic belief system from the ancient Middle East and predated Christianity by several centuries.

In the early 1970s, the Chicago Tribune interviewed De'Arechaga, and he explained to the interviewer that he considered himself to be of the old religion. He further explained that he opened his shop as a safe space for local witches and warlocks to perform their rituals. The name he chose for the shop, El-Sabarum, which meant, 'many gods' reflected his desire to welcome those involved in the old ways.

During the interview, De'Arechaga stated that the release of the movie, *The Exorcist* had a severely negative impact on his business. While the residents of the neighborhood were welcoming to his store, several Christian churches considered him and his clientele to be Satanists. It wasn't uncommon to find people praying that God would rid him and his shop from the neighborhood. Whether or not it worked, De'Arechaga eventually closed his shop and moved on. Today, the Tonic Room is no longer known for catering to witches and occult rituals. Rather, it's a fun, artist-friendly establishment hosting local bands, comedians and DJs. Nevertheless, this has not stopped the Tonic Room from being known for its many ghosts.

Since opening the bar, there have been several unexplained, and some might even say, sinister encounters with the ghosts of the building's colorful past. On the second floor that was used as a brothel, men have reported the sensation of being touched by unseen hands in a sexually suggestive manner. And the apparitions of prostitutes and gangsters have been witnessed in the dark corners of the bar area. The apparitions have been described in various ways, but the most common are reported as rough-looking men with scantily clad prostitutes sitting on their laps. The strangest, and sinister, incident has nothing to do with the specters of gangsters but rather, a dagger.

During the renovations of the basement, workers found a worn looking dagger resting on a window well. After it was removed a bar employee went down to the basement and fell on the floor where the pentagram was found and went catatonic. When he was discovered by the owner, he seemed unable to move or communicate. He was rushed to the hospital and following an intensive examination, the doctor said he could find nothing wrong with him. When he recovered from the trance-like state, he said he remembered nothing. After the bizarre incident, the owners put the dagger back where it was found.

If you're looking for live music in an eclectic atmosphere, the Tonic Room is the place to find it. However, I caution you, don't go anywhere near the basement. It's off-limits to anyone not on staff. And to anyone who doesn't understand the bizarre power in it.

# Chapter 21: That Steak Joynt

When the paranormal became mainstream in the early 2000s, businesses in many cities that had histories with hauntings were reluctant to be known for such a dubious distinction. With that being said, the curiously named, That Steak Joynt in Chicago, wore that distinction as a badge of honor. And will go down as being one of the most frighteningly haunted eating establishments in the history of the windy city.

Long before the building on North Wells was That Steak Joynt, it was Piper's Bakery in the 1860s. When the great Chicago fire of 1871 tore through the city leaving destruction in its wake including Piper's Bakery, Henry Piper refused to be defeated. He worked day and night to rebuild his business on the same site as the original. Piper made his bakery bigger and more profitable and continued to be a neighborhood fixture for another 60 years.

Following the closing of Piper's Bakery, a variety of businesses set up shop, a laundry, and hardware store were two that stated the longest. Strangely enough, none of these businesses ever complained of ghosts terrifying their clientele and their workers. That didn't appear to happen until That Steak Joynt took up residence. The original owners, Ralph Mitchell, and Harold Seltzer were too busy to notice anything strange when they bought the building in 1962. However, the following owners, Billy Siegel, and Raudell Perez were the first to report something out of the ordinary was going on in their restaurant.

When Perez and Mitchell converted the bakery case into a bar, they placed the marble bust of a grinning peasant gripping a wine glass above the bar. The bust which came from the Matson Steamship line not only appeared to have a mind of its own but also seemed to possess special powers.

According to several customers, if you stared at the bust long enough the expression on the marble peasant's face would change. One minute it appeared to be grinning and the next it appeared to frown. As for its special abilities, a local stockbroker claimed it gave him winning stock tips while others claimed it healed illness. Interestingly when a local paranormal investigator took pictures of the bust, two streaks of white spirit energy emanated from the bust.

Reportedly, the marble bust of the peasant wasn't the only haunted decoration in the restaurant. Hanging on the wall on the staircase were the portraits of William Devine and his wife, Catherine. William, an immigrant from Ireland, came to Chicago and made a successful career as a milk merchant. While The portrait of William was quiet, the portrait of his wife was an altogether different matter. It was said that if you stared at the portrait for too long you might find yourself becoming physically ill. The complaints go to be so bad the painting had to be removed and was bought by a local merchant.

When reports of ghosts and hauntings became too numerous to ignore, several seances were held in the 1980s. During one session the medium, Robert Dubeil, claimed to come into contact with the three spirits that haunted the building. One of the spirits claimed to be the architect that the designed the building. The second spirit said it was a female customer who frequented the building when it was a bakery. As for the third, it appeared to be the spirit of a double homicide victim from the turn of the 20th century. The murderer was never caught. One of the attendees, a Chicago Sun Times reported became so violently ill she needed to be removed.

Before Raudell Perez passed, he reported that he had a difficult time keeping the restaurant adequately staffed due to all the spirit activity. The night cleaning crew were the hardest to keep because no one wanted to be in the building after dark. One night a janitor came face to face with one of the spectral denizens of the building. He was so frightened by what he saw, he promptly ran out of the building leaving it unsecured. He never returned to the building even to pick up his final paycheck.

The owners, themselves, had the occasional run-in with the ghosts that haunted the restaurant. Raudell Perez, often stayed late to do the bookkeeping because the building was quiet after hours. As he sat at the bar, out of the corner of his eye, he watched as two apparitions suddenly appeared and started walking up the stairs. Perez jumped off the barstool and quickly followed the mysterious figures up the stairs. When he got to the top of the stairs he watched as the couple vanished. When he returned to the bar he asked the cleaning crew if they had seen the people who walked up the stairs. They, of course, answered, no.

The hauntings at That Steak Joynt, appear to be a mixture of both the benevolent and malevolent. And the malevolent appears to be winning. Numerous employees have reported being physically assaulted by an aggressive spirit as they worked. One frightening supernatural episode involved a female worker who was clearing and washing dishes. After setting a stack of dishes in the sink, she claimed that a rough hand grabbed her wrist and squeezed. When she turned around to face her attacker she was shocked to see she was alone.

Following the terrifying encounter, the young tried to leave and the rough hand seized her again this time dragging her across the floor. She desperately tried to fight her attacker off but she couldn't fight what she couldn't see. Not knowing what else to do, she let out an ear-piercing scream. Perez and a waiter ran into the room and found the poor young woman passed out on the floor. When she came to, through hysterical tears she explained what had happened to her and showed her rescuers the welts that formed on her wrists. Perez sent her home and she quit the next day.

A few years ago That Steak Joynt closed and Adobo Mexican Grill opened up, serving the neighborhood fine Mexican cuisine. They didn't last long, but when questioned the owners said they never experienced anything the likes of what their predecessors reported. Time will tell if the next occupants deal with the malevolent entire a haunting the building.

# Chapter 22: The Irish Legend

Archer Avenue, a long stretch of road that runs through the south side of Chicago, is famous for being home to the city's most well-known ghost, Ressurection Mary. However, on South Archer Avenue, in the suburb of Willow Springs is one of Chicago's lesser known haunts, The Irish Legend. A former speakeasy and brothel that houses the ghosts of the south side's troubled history with organized crime.

In the 1840s, with the building of the Michigan canal, a huge influx of German and Irish immigrants arrived looking for work. These tireless men built the canal and stockyards and eventually called the area home. In the 1880s and 1890s, more construction followed and small communities became thriving cities along Archer Avenue. One unfortunate outcome of the construction, several Native American burial mounds which are common across the Midwest, were disturbed and destroyed. Many accept this as a viable reason why the area has gained such a reputation for being haunted.

The Irish Legend, as it is now called, was built sometime around 1900, as a place for the hardworking men of the area to get a few drinks after work. The Irish Legend was just the first of many pubs and taverns that eventually would pop up along Archer Avenue in the early days of the 20th century. And, of course with this being Chicago, organized crime wanted a piece of the action.

When prohibition became the law of the land and the sale of alcohol was outlawed, the majority of the pubs and taverns closed its doors and shuttered their windows. Except for The Irish Legend. The bar stayed open and became one of the biggest speakeasies on the south side. The basement and attic were used for drinking and gambling. The second floor was partitioned into numerous small rooms where the ladies of the night entertained their gentlemen callers. The Irish Legend was more successful as an illegal operation than when it was a legitimate business.

Like with most places that enjoyed the Irish Legend's reputation, violent death would soon follow. One of the stories concerned a bartender and his forbidden love affair with one of the prostitutes. When the manager learned of what was going on under his roof, he lured the bartender to the basement and crushed his skull. The ghost of the brutally murdered bartender makes his presence known by knocking over beer barrels and pushing over whoever is brave enough to enter his domain.

Another story concerns one of the prostitutes who was brutally slain by a couple of wiseguys when she refused their advances. The beat her death and wrapped her lifeless body in a rug. When they realized they wouldn't be able to dispose of her body until the place was closed, they stored the rug in the dining room. Legend says the girl's blood seeped out of the rug staining the floor. The stain that is still there is said to be impossible to clean.

Back in the day before legal abortions, it was common in houses of ill repute to perform abortions on the prostitutes if the became unexpectedly pregnant. At the Irish Legend, the abortions were typically performed by disgraced doctors in the kitchen area and because of the unsafe and unsanitary conditions, it wasn't uncommon for the girls to die. In the kitchen area, the apparitions of angry young women have been witnessed by staff. Employees have also reported the eerie disembodied crying of babies followed by an intense feeling of loss.

On the back stairs of the building, the sounds of fighting between men have been heard. These back stairs were used as a means to sneak prominent citizens into the building as well as smuggling dead bodies out. Numerous people disappeared down those stairs never to be seen again.

The Irish Legend in the south side community of Willow Springs is a reminder of the violence that characterized Chicago's troubled past. The Irish Legend is still open for business and it's ghosts never rest.

# Chapter 23: Marshall Field Jr. House

Long before the first million-dollar homes went up, and Chicago's exclusive North Shore towns and neighborhoods were nothing more than small farming communities. The elite of Chicago society resided in a six-block, south side neighborhood in what is now known as Chicago's Prairie Avenue Historical District. And the wealthiest family on Prairie Avenue was the family of Marshall Field.

If there was a reigning king of Chicago in the late 1800s and early 1900s, department store tycoon and entrepreneur, Marshall Field would have been it. And, although Marshall Field and his family were respected pillars of Chicago society, they were not free from scandal. And that scandal was caused by the alleged accidental death of his eldest son and heir to the empire, Marshall Field, Jr.

Since his untimely and suspicious death in 1905, the official story of the death of Marshall Field, Jr was as follows. One afternoon, while preparing for a hunting expedition, Field shot himself while cleaning his hunting rifle. When he was discovered, Field was rushed to Mercy hospital where he perished from his injuries five days later. Marshall Field Jr, a 38-year-old loving husband, and father of three small children was dead as a result of a tragic accident. Or was he?

The life of Marshall Field, Jr was not as innocent as many people thought. Apparently, Field had a dark side, a secret life he did his best to keep hidden. And it was after his death that his dark side came into the light of day. It was this secret life that may have killed him.

According to friends and business associates, Marshall Field, Jr indulged in the sins of the flesh with the ladies of the night. On several occasions, Field Jr was seen coming and going from the Everleigh Club, an exclusive brothel on nearby Dearborn Street. And it wasn't just the hookers, Field Jr, had a gambling addiction that resulted in him owing large amounts of money to local bookies.

The popular theory concerning the death of Marshall Field Jr was that he was shot and killed by his debtors at the brothel. Knowing how powerful his family was, the murderers dragged his body back to his home at 1919 South Prairie Avenue. When they got in they set up the body to make it look like Field Jr died by his own hand.

When the incident was investigated by the police, the owners of the brothel, the Everleigh sisters were questioned. They, of course, denied the story saying it was fabricated by their competitors to put a black mark on their establishment. Having the son of the wealthiest man in Chicago die in their club would certainly put a huge dent in their client list.

Whether it was an accidental shooting or bad guys collecting on a gambling debt, the official story reported in newspapers was death by misadventure. Following his death, the house at 1919 South Prairie Avenue was shuttered and remained empty for decades.

Today, 1919 South Prairie Avenue is home to luxury condominiums. And like the rest of the Prairie Avenue District, it was declared a Chicago landmark and placed on the National Register of Historic Places. And according to some of the residents of the Marshall Field Jr House, his ghost is still very much active.

Those who have had encounters with the Field empire heir say that he appears as a shadow that walks the hallways. The apparition is also said to be accompanied by a cold breeze and a feeling of sorrow. Others have reported the sounds of people struggling to carry a body, giving credence to the story he was killed at the brothel and brought home by the men that killed him.

Whether or not Marshall Field Jr, was killed at home or not, just taking a walk down Prairie Avenue will transport you back to the gilded age of the Windy City.

# Section 2: Welcome To Illinois, Come For The Hospitality - Stay For The Weirdness

Welcome to Illinois, come for the hospitality - stay for the weirdness is something that I've been saying for years about the great State of Illinois. A state I love and a state I call home. In this state, depending on where you go, you will experience that great Midwestern hospitality that we are famous for. One other thing you may discover, the Land of Lincoln is easily one of the weirdest states in the United States of America.

From the busy streets of our largest city, Chicago in the north, all the way down to the southernmost tip of the state, an area called 'Little Egypt' you may just find any kind of weirdness your heart desires. We have homes still haunted by spirits of slaves from days long since passed, to small-town cops chasing a UFO across several counties. We even have a cave that just may prove our nation was explored by the ancient peoples of Egypt and the Middle East thousands of years before Christopher Columbus and his famous voyage. All we have to do now is just rediscover the damned thing.

So, if you're looking for a state to kick back in and perhaps search for the strange and unusual, then Illinois is most definitely for you. So, again I say, welcome to Illinois, come for the hospitality - stay for the weirdness. You won't be disappointed.

# Chapter 1: Williamsburg Hill

All over the world, there are locations that, for whatever reason, have a mystical quality about them. Places that are known for such potent positive energy that people come by the thousands in that hope that may experience that power for themselves. From Lourdes in France, with its miraculous healing waters. To Glastonbury, England, that is believed to be the final resting place of Arthur, King of the Britons. And the doorway to Annwn of Welsh mythology, the mythical kingdom of the Fey. These mysterious places are considered sacred by millions and seem to benefit mankind.

As with any places of positive energy, there must be places that are the polar opposite. Locations that have always been just bad, for the lack of a better word. One such place that radiates bad energy just so happens to be right here in the prairie state. A place so bad, very few would dare to tread, Williamsburg Hill.

Rising 810 feet over the central Illinois towns of Shelbyville and Tower Hill, Williamsburg Hill is quite possibly the spookiest place in Illinois. Over the years there have been numerous encounters with terrifying ghosts, strange creatures, and sightings of UFOs. No one can pin down why this seemingly innocent hill has such a bad atmosphere. Some offer the theory that it has always been negatively charged. This could explain why the local Native Tribes avoid it all costs, believing it to be the abode to evil spirits. Others believe it was cursed when white settlers arrived and claimed the land as their own. This has been a common theme running throughout the history of the United States.

In 1839, the village of Tower Hill was founded by a medical doctor, Thomas Williams. When Williams arrived in the area he began setting up his town. He was approached by the local Native American tribes who sternly warned him the hill and surrounding area wasn't fit for human habitation. Williams listened to their frightening tales of spirits and strange lights that flew around the hill. And like most white settlers of the day, Williams, completely disregarded what they had to say.

For over forty years, Tower Hill was a dream come true for Doc Williams and his family. The town grew to an impressive population of well over 2,000 people. At that time 2,000 was considered a bustling metropolis for a Midwestern town on the plains. And the town's prosperity gave owed its success to it being on one of the busiest stagecoach routes in the United States. The rich and famous arrived on the stagecoach, drank in the town's many saloons, and filled up the rooms of the local hotels. But that would all soon change.

The fortunes of the town began to suffer in 1881 when the stagecoach line was retired and replaced by the railroad, which completely bypassed the town. The days of wine and roses were over for the towns of Tower Hill and Shelbyville. The rich and famous no longer came to town, the hotels were empty except for drifters and the saloons fell silent.

For many years Tower Hill was a virtual ghost town, a mere shadow of its former days. The population dwindled until the mid 20th century when people seeking a quieter life began moving back. It's at this time the residents began noticing something about the hill wasn't quite right. Even frightening.

Much of the bizarre activity on the hill seems to come from Ridge Cemetery, a disused graveyard near the top of the hill. Ridge Cemetery is the final resting place of some of the earliest residents of the area. Over time, nature has begun reclaiming the cemetery and probably would have been forgotten had it not been for two factors, rampant vandalism of the tombstones and the terrifying hauntings said to occur there.

One of the apparitions believed to haunt Ridge Cemetery is the specter of a crazed old man. Visitors have reported the apparition suddenly appearing and screaming at people to leave. He then vanishes before making physical contact with the stunned witness. A phantom funeral procession is said to walk up the hill, complete with coffin, priest, and mourners. Those who have witnessed this solemn event say the procession disappears as it enters the cemetery.

Perhaps the most disturbing spirit encounter in the cemetery concerns a mystified mother and her emotionally scarred little girl. As the woman drove past the cemetery, her little girl in the back seat began to cry uncontrollably. When she managed to calm her little girl down, she asked her what upset her. The little girl replied that black-robed ghosts surrounded the car and said to her, "Come stay with us underground.". According to the woman, her daughter had nightmares for weeks following the encounter.

If stories of lost souls and vengeful wraiths on the hill aren't enough to scare you, Williamsburg Hill has a couple of creepy monsters that call this place home. A tall, hairy bipedal monster has been seen on the forested hill. Hikers have been startled by fleeting glimpses of the beast as it appeared to follow them from a distance. Fortunately, for the lone hiker, the Bigfoot-like creature appears to be merely curious and doesn't seem to mean any harm. Yet.

The second beast said to live on the hill is one that is found in the folklore of European and Asian countries. In the early days, a creature that can only be described as a dragon has been witnessed flying around the hill. The local Tribes have stories of a fearsome monster that lives on the hill and was known to swoop down and carry off warriors. The dragon, assuming it exists at all, has not been seen for well over a century.

Williamsburg Hill appears to attract visitors from far away worlds as well. Lights and unexplained aircraft have been seen circling the hill. These UFOs have led some to believe that an alien base is hidden inside the cave and all the paranormal activity is a means to keep people away. One witness reported watching as a bright red light descended from the sky and land on the hill. A few moments later the red light lifted off the hill, passing over his car causing it to sputter and die.

Williamsburg appears to be a place of high strangeness. High strangeness is a term used by researchers to attempt and classify activity that seems to incorporate hauntings, creatures, and aliens. If it is, Williamsburg Hill may be a vortex area where strange things can come and go at will, making this Illinois landmark one frightening place to visit.

# Chapter 2: Greenwood Cemetery

Throughout my time in school, history was one of those subjects that just seemed to come to life for me. I'm sure this is why I put so much emphasis on historical research as a paranormal investigator. And the American Civil War was my favorite subject, which brings us to Decatur, Illinois and it's haunted graveyard, Greenwood Cemetery.

Decatur is believed by many researchers to be one of the most haunted towns in the Midwest. Several buildings and homes in this quaint small town are known to boast a ghost or two. As a researcher, I don't usually buy into the belief that if something is built over a Native American burial ground that automatically makes it haunted. However, I'm willing to make an exception where Decatur is concerned.

If you're not willing to entertain the Native American burial ground theory, then perhaps the hauntings could be due to Greenwood Cemetery. According to the historical record, Greenwood Cemetery wasn't officially incorporated until 1857. Nevertheless, it is believed that burials as early as 1820 took place here. And it was the war between the States that made this unassuming and pleasant cemetery so haunted.

Civil War tore the country down the middle. Camp Douglas, which has a chapter in the previous section, was the prison camp located just outside Chicago. Thousands of captured Confederate soldiers were incarcerated in this abysmal prison camp. Decatur, Illinois was along the prison train route that carried prisoners of war to the camp. It was a common practice that if a prisoner was sick or dead their bodies were dumped.

Stories abound that the prison train would roll to a stop and the dead were carted off and hastily buried in unmarked graves. However, not all the prisoners who were buried at Greenwood were dead. According to Union soldiers that spoke up after the War, if a Confederate soldier was alive, but on the verge of death, they were shot or just buried alive. Such atrocities may be why Greenwood Cemetery is so haunted.

One of the haunted hotspots in Greenwood Cemetery is no longer there. In 1967, the public Mausoleum was torn down due to its age and poor condition. When it was standing, anguished cries would echo throughout the structure. And unexplained lights were seen at night moving throughout the Mausoleum. Mourners who came to pay their respects would often complain of phantom footsteps and the uncomfortable feeling of being watched.

Ghost lights have been a part of the spiritual lore of various cultures all over the world. From the 'corpse candles' of British folklore to the Marfa and Brown mountain lights in the United States, people have been seeing these inexplicable lights for centuries. Mainstream science suggests this anomaly is by no means ghostly in nature. They argue these lights are combustible gases escaping from decaying matter and tectonic stress. While this may be true in most cases, people who have experienced the Greenwood lights would differ in their opinion.

A number of years ago, Decatur experienced a devastating flood. The waters caused the ground of the cemetery to become so soft that it washed graves away. Witnesses of the lights believe these intelligent acting light anomalies are the souls of the dead searching for their bodies. The lights are interesting and all, but it's the apparitions that are the true hallmark of Greenwood Cemetery.

In the 1970s, a local man was visiting the Civil War section when a strange sight caught his eye. Standing in the middle of the section was a dirty, bearded man wearing the tattered gray uniform of the Confederacy. Bravely, he approached the out of place man who appeared to be confused and disoriented. He asked if the odd man was ok, and if not, could he help. The soldier turned to the man with tears in his eyes and replied, "I just wanna go home." The man then watched as the soldier melted into thin air.

Greenwood Cemetery is a location that has become a favorite among local ghost hunters. Having been investigated numerous times, they have determined that it is without a doubt haunted by its tragic past. If only a handful of these stories are true, I believe it.

# Chapter 3: Cops Vs Aliens

Law enforcement officials are well known for being skeptical. They have to be because on a day to day basis they are dealing with people who lie, cheat, and steal. Being skeptical and practicing critical thinking is nothing short of a job requirement. Police officers, when on and off the job, are highly skilled, highly trained observers. A big part of their job is observing people's actions and reactions. Dealing with the abnormal is not something they like doing. Nevertheless, every so often, the police are the first people that deal with something that goes beyond human understanding. In January 2000, several police officers across several towns found themselves in a situation that was not of this world.

In the early morning hours of January 5, Melvern Noll, a local businessman was working his second job as a delivery man. Having finished his rounds, Noll stopped at his business, a mini-golf course to check on its security. Before entering the building his attention was drawn to an unusually bright star in the northern sky. Not giving it a second thought, he unlocked the door and walked in.

After a few minutes of checking on the building, Noll walked back outside and noticed that the unusually bright light he dismissed as a star, seemed to be brighter and closer. And it was doing something stars don't do, it was slowly moving quietly across the sky. And then Melvern Noll, came face to face with the unthinkable. The light was attached to a much larger object. An object completely unlike anything he'd ever seen.

The craft he had in his sights was rectangular in shape. Noll said the craft had windows along the side and appeared to be much larger than a house. Noll watched as the craft glided away silently eventually disappearing over the horizon. Shaken by what he just witnessed, Melvern Noll, jumped in his truck and did what most people might do in a similar situation, he reported it to the police.

At 4:15 AM, officer Ed Barton received a call from his dispatcher he thought he'd never hear. He was advised they had received several calls from people reporting unexplained lights in the sky above Horner Park. Understandably, Barton was dubious about the call and joked with his dispatcher about crackpots and little green men. But, investigating such things was a part of the job, and despite his own beliefs, he quickly made his way to the scene.

As Barton approached Horner Park, he could see two brilliant light hovering over the park. When the lights began moving away from the park he dutifully followed not believing what he was seeing. His first thought was that someone had to be playing a prank of some kind, but he found himself driving faster to keep up. When he got close enough to see the hovering object, he could tell this was no joke. After his eyes adjusted to the light, he could see the lights were attached to a much larger, triangle-shaped craft. Barton watched in shocked disbelief as the object turned and began to slowly move away. It glided silently and was picking up speed.

While Barton followed the object, he contacted his dispatcher and discovered he wasn't the only officer in pursuit of the object. Several officers from nearby Lebanon, Millstadt, and Shiloh had been following the craft before Benton joined the chase. As the officers pursued the object, they remained in constant contact with each other and their respective dispatches. Such comments as, "It's huge" and "V-shaped craft" filled the police scanners in those early morning hours. One officer observed the craft was a mere 500 feet off the ground and could make it out in greater detail through binoculars. The officers finally broke off the chase when the craft moved to the west, crossing the state line to Missouri and vanishing.

To this day, the officers involved in the chase with the strange craft are still unsure of what they pursued that morning. Their rational mindset tells them that what they saw had to be some kind of secret military aircraft. But, when Scott Air Force base was contacted, they denied having anything in the air that night. And they saw nothing on the radar that should not have been there. The great southern Illinois UFO chase has gone down as being one of the best documented UFO cases in the history of modern UFOlogy. And it was all documented by trained, professional observers, the police.

# Chapter 4: The White Cemetery

If you were to ask someone to name a haunted cemetery in the Chicagoland area, their first response would probably be Bachelors Grove, the famously haunted cemetery on the city's south side. On the city's north side, located in the affluent town of North Barrington, is another haunted cemetery. A cemetery just as active with spirit energy as it's south side counterpart, The White Cemetery. Located along the peaceful and unassuming Cuba Road, the White Cemetery is surrounded by the large homes of the wealthy community. It is almost unthinkable that such a town with its squeaky clean image would play host to a cemetery that is such a notorious haunt. However, the history of this village in Lake County is anything but squeaky clean.

Throughout the 1920 and 1930s, Lake County, Illinois was a well-known playground for Chicago's criminal elite. Chicago's very own king of the underworld, Al Capone, vacationed in the area as well as hiding out there when things in the city got too hot for him. Several old homes and businesses can lay claim to the dubious distinction, Al Capone slept here. When it comes to the haunted history of the White Cemetery, the majority of the residents of North Barrington would like to keep the rumors of ghosts hush-hush. Nevertheless, this has not stopped the myriad of stories that have arisen over the last three decades about the haunted cemetery. Despite all their best efforts, they can't keep a good ghost down.

Many who venture down Cuba Road have reported large balls of light and misty apparitions in the gates of the cemetery. Several have even reported the spirits leaving its confines and wandering Cuba Road. One of the spirits is that of an elderly woman who walks on the side of the road. When people stop to inquire if she needs help, the seemingly sweet little old lady lets out a horrific ear-piercing cackling laugh. She disappears leaving the unwitting good Samaritan in a state of shock.

It's not just the cemetery that is haunted, Cuba Road appears to have its fair share of frightening phantoms. Those taking a drive down the road have reported seeing the image of a cigar-chomping gangster suddenly appear in their back seat. While others have reported being chased by a vintage, black sedan that vanishes just as suddenly as it appears.

Lastly, like it's south side counterpart, a spectral white farmhouse is said to appear on Cuba Road. But unlike the phantom farmhouse that appears in the woods around Bachelors Grove, this house actually existed. In the 1950s, a farmhouse burned to the ground killing the family of twelve that lived in it. Those who have seen the house reported an eerie blue haze surrounding it and 12 ghostly figures standing on the front porch beckoning the witness to come and join them. To that, I say no thanks.

Several researchers regard the stories about White Cemetery to be nothing more than a pure urban legend. However, the stories persist and many credible eyewitnesses have reported encounters with the unknown on Cuba Road and in the White Cemetery.

# Chapter 5: Burrow's Cave

"In fourteen hundred and ninety-two, Columbus sailed the ocean blue." If you were a child in the American public school system chances are this catchy little tune about Christopher Columbus' voyage to the new world was drilled into your brain for all time. For many years it was believed that Columbus was the first white European to set foot anywhere near the North American continent. And we bought it because it was all we ever knew. What if I told you Columbus wasn't the first European to set foot on the North American continent? What if others came long before him?

Over the last 50 years, several discoveries have been made that could potentially refute what we've all been taught in school. The Kensington runestone was unearthed in a Minnesota farmer's field and just may prove that Vikings penetrated the vast forests of the American Midwest. Several pieces of jewelry were dug up in Tennessee that depicts Hebrew writing. Lastly, a megalithic structure in New Hampshire called, 'Mystery Hill' is a popular destination for curiosity seekers who believe it was built by 6th-century Irish explorers. Of course, skeptics immediately dismiss these discoveries as hoaxes, stating that these ancient cultures couldn't sail the Atlantic ocean in the boats they used. Nevertheless, these anomalous discoveries were made and they challenge history as we know it. One of these discoveries was made right here in my home state of Illinois. A discovery that just may prove ancient cultures visited our shores thousands of years ago.

In the summer of 1982, cave explorer Russell Burrows was walking along a path near the Little Wabash River. A path he walked many times and knew well. After tripping over a rock, Burrows, found himself falling into a cave he never noticed before. Shaking himself off and checking himself for injuries, Burrows discovered himself in a large cavern. Such caverns were not uncommon, but it was the contents of the cave that mystified him. He discovered mummified bodies and thousands of black stones with writing on them he wasn't familiar with. Burrows concluded that whatever this place was these relics should not be here.

As Burrows went deeper into the cavern, he discovered carvings on the wall of faces that could only be described as African in appearance. He also found carvings of elephants, lions, and gorillas, animals that were not indigenous to the United States. To Burrows, he had just made the greatest discovery of his lifetime. A discovery that could potentially prove the ancients found a way to traverse the violent tides of the Atlantic ocean thousands of years before the commonly accepted theories.

When Burrows presented the black stones to the experts, he was told that the markings were of various ancient languages: Egyptian, Punic, Libyan, and Arabic. Although this was an impressive find, the experts instantly called foul when Burrows explained where they were found. They sharply criticized the find saying they were obvious hoaxes, as the languages inscribed on them made no sense in the language they came from. And there was absolutely no way these cultures visited our continent. They also floated the idea that the stones may have been left by a hobbyist who forgot about them. Personally, I can accept the idea of a hoax, but the latter theory is a bit of a stretch.

Undaunted by the findings of the mainstream scientific community, Burrows received a much different opinion by another set of academics. These researchers theorized that the languages on the stones may represent a root language. An ancient tongue all these other languages were based on. They further stated that the carvings of the warriors and animals were consistent with their country of origin. These carvings were either made in haste or were inscribed using substandard tools.

Years after the cave's discovery, Russell Burrows and Fred Rydholm authored the book *The Mystery Cave Of Many Faces*. In the book, the authors wrote that ancient travelers from Egypt and Middle Eastern countries sailed up the Mississippi and settled in southern Illinois. They theorized further that due to the harshness of the environment, these ancient explorers died and their bodies and personal belongings were interred in the caves. The book was panned by the mainstream scientific community and was considered mere fantasy.

Was Burrows' discovery a hoax as suggested by the mainstream scientific community? Or, were the artifacts discovered in the cave truly of ancient origin placed there by unlikely explorers? No one can really say, because the cave is a closely guarded secret known by a select few people. And they aren't talking.

# Chapter 6: The O'Hare Airport UFO

Chicago's O'Hare International Airport is one of the United States' busiest airports. Hundred of flights, national and international, come and go daily. Among this dizzying array of flights, something was witnessed over O'Hare in 2006, that could make this airport the busiest in our solar system.

On November 7, 2006, at 4:30 PM, several airport employees, including flight crews, were dumbfounded when a large saucer-shaped object hovering over gate C-17 suddenly appeared. The airport was alarmed by the peculiar object and immediately rerouted planes to other airports and grounded flights preparing to depart. Airport officials wanted to get to the bottom of the strange craft that unexpectedly appeared in its airspace. The mysterious craft in question, stuck around for approximately five minutes until it abruptly vanished. Several local news agencies reported on the UFO sighting causing a minor stir. This was a mere five years after terrorists brought down the World Trade Center and anything strange in the skies over a major city was a cause for concern.

As with anything from the realm of the fantastic, the UFO was immediately explained away. The experts blamed cloud formation and bizarre atmospheric anomalies, you know, the usual suspects. However, eyewitnesses are adamant in saying that what they saw was an anomaly of the nuts and bolts variety. They were convinced that what they saw was a legitimate spacecraft of unknown origin. And no expert could tell them otherwise.

# Chapter 7: The Farmer City Monster

Bigfoot is the mysterious ape-like creature made famous by its many sightings in the heavily forested and mountainous regions of the Pacific Northwest. And although similar creatures known by different names have been seen across the United States, Illinois boasts more sightings of this beast east of the Mississippi. Whatever this creature is, whether a crazed hairy human or living fossil that supposedly went extinct at the end of the last Ice Age, it seems to call the woods and hills of southern Illinois home. In the Spring of 1970, one of these hirsute creatures kept the community of Farmer City, Illinois on edge.

In the Spring of 1970, a farmer awakened one morning to a horrific sight. Some unknown, bloodthirsty beast tore three of his sheep to pieces. Distraught over the slaughter, the farmer contacted the Sheriff's office and a deputy was immediately dispatched. After thoroughly investigating the scene, the deputy told the farmer he needed to better secure his animals as they were obviously killed by a pack of wild dogs. Little did the deputy know how wrong he was.

A couple of months following the slaughter of the sheep, a group of local teenagers were parked at a local 'lover's lane' near Salt Creek. As the friends were laughing and drinking, they suddenly became aware that they were being watched and an odorous stench filled the air. Wanting to get a better look, one of the boys turned on their headlights and they all received the scare of their young lives. Staring at them from just beyond the tree line was a tall, hairy humanoid creature with piercing yellow eyes. When the girls let out a bloodcurdling scream, the creature turned and hurriedly rushed into the surrounding woods. The young women were so terrified they demanded their male companions take them home immediately, date night at Salt Creek having been interrupted by the inexplicable.

After taking their girlfriends home, the boys returned and encountered the creature a second time. As they sat in their car with the windows rolled up, the stench of the creature permeated the car, and they watched as a huge shadow lurked among the trees. The boys left to get the police and the only thing the police found was what appeared to be a nest made up of leaves and tree limbs. They didn't see the creature, however, the strong odor remained hanging heavily in the air.

Three weeks following the Salt Creek sighting, several sightings of the creature were made in the general vicinity of Farmer City. One of the witnesses, Robert Hayslip, a local police officer watched in awe as the tall creature walked directly in front of his patrol car. A week later, a pair of hikers saw the creature bathing in a river. At first, they thought it was a bear looking for food. That was until it stood up on its hind legs and rushed into the woods when it realized it was being observed.

Following the report of the hikers, conservation officers investigated the area around the river. They were shocked when they discovered large humanlike tracks near the muddy edge of the river. Falling back on their many years of experience with the animals that lived in the woods, they concluded that whatever this animal was, it was not a bear.

The encounters with the creature continued as it seemed to be migrating northwest. A group of construction workers outside Waynesville, witnessed the creature run across the road as they drove to work in the early morning hours. The last known sighting was made by Waynesville resident who said he saw the creature in his backyard. After that sighting the Farmer City Monster vanished, never to be seen again.

Skeptics are typically quick in dismissing reports of a large, hairy bipedal animal as nothing more than misidentified animals. And although they're right in an overwhelming majority of reports, reports of the Farmer City Monster were made by dozens of credible witnesses. Police officers, conservation officers, and residents who had nothing to gain by reporting the creature stand by their claims. Whatever the creature was, it has yet to return.

# Chapter 8: The Grass Lake Encounters

High strangeness is a phenomenon in the paranormal generally associated with UFOs and related phenomena. However, during these bizarre occurrences, poltergeist activity, strange electrical disturbances, and sightings of otherworldly creatures make high strangeness, well, strange. In my home state of Illinois, in the 1970s, there was a case of high strangeness that terrified all who experienced it. The bizarre events that transpired in the quiet northern Illinois community of Grass Lake lasted for two years, driving all those who experienced to the brink of madness.

Like many reports of paranormal activity, the Grass Lake encounters began simply. On a warm summer night, the local police and fire departments began receiving reports of large orange balls of light dancing in the skies above the small lakeside community. The police were at a complete loss of what to do concerning the reports. Nevertheless, they had a job to do and responded.

When the police arrived to investigate the reports, they saw nothing out of the ordinary. Not a single ball of light was seen in the sky. Although the police found nothing, this did not stop the residents searching for answers. The day after the initial sightings, the residents of Grass Lake contacted both UFO and new age groups. They hoped these groups could give them some insight into what they experienced. Shortly after contacting these groups, the mysterious activity went from merely seeing balls of light and became something far more sinister. To the families of Grass Lake, Illinois, it seemed that something evil was unleashed upon their community.

As the frightening activity unfolded, one resident, Mrs. H, kept a journal detailing what she and her family were experiencing. One journal entry made by Mrs. H talked about the visitation of a large menacing black shadow entity that appeared in her bedroom late one night. At first, she thought it was her husband until she turned on the lights and it vanished leaving a feeling of dread in its wake.

A great deal of the activity appeared to be focused on the H home, and other residents reported frightening activity in their homes. At various times hairy creatures were witnessed skulking about the exterior of the homes. And whatever these creatures were they believed to leave long deep scratches on the siding of the houses and three-toed footprints in the soft dirt. All residents experienced poltergeist phenomena in their homes. Plates and glasses seemed to take on a life of their own by leaping from shelves and hovering around the house. Disturbing disembodied voices were heard and dark reptilian shapes were seen darting around from room to room in homes. The strangest activity was yet to come.

The homeowners that saw the balls of light reported the weirdest activity of all. In defiance of gravity, their homes jumped off the ground and floated for several seconds in the air. As the activity intensified, the residents called the police only to be told the police had no jurisdiction over such matters. If the police could do nothing, who could? Enter legendary paranormal investigator and author, Dennis William Hauck.

When Hauck arrived, he immediately visited the H residence as they appeared to receive the brunt of the activity. While Hauck interviewed Mrs. H and went over her journal, everyone in attendance was startled by what sounded like a heavy sledgehammer striking the side of the home rattling the walls. Hauck ran outside to investigate whether or not someone was playing a prank, he found nothing. What he did find backed up the claims of the Grass Lake residents. Deep gouge marks ran along the siding left by some unknown agent with three very sharp claws.

After spending a week in Grass Lake, Hauck got into his car and experienced electrical disturbances commonly associated with a close encounter with a UFO. The interior and exterior lights began to rapidly flash and the radio let out a loud ear-piercing whine. When he finally got the car started, he took it to a local mechanic who said the car appeared to be in perfect working condition. The only thing that defied logic was the driver's door somehow became magnetized and was drawing shop tools towards it. And a Geiger counter Hauck left in his trunk was broken beyond repair. Hauck came to the conclusion that whatever this mysterious power was that plagued the good people of Grass Lake, Illinois was very real and quite possibly dangerous.

Three years after the investigation, Hauck returned to Grass Lake and met once again with Mrs. H. The woman who was once friendly and thoughtful was now sullen and depressed. Mrs. H told the investigator that following his departure, she suffered a nervous breakdown and her husband walked out on her. She further stated that her family disowned her because they considered crazy and a liar. Mrs. H, lost her battle with the sinister alien forces that laid siege on her house. The lights and activity may be gone, but Grass Lake is still there, hoping the bizarre activity never returns.

# Chapter 9: The Macomb Poltergeist

In the field of paranormal research and investigation, no activity invites more fear and dread than the mysterious poltergeist. This terrifying activity is characterized by heavy poundings on walls, disturbances of physical objects, and property destruction. As far as this inexplicable activity is concerned there seem to be more questions than answers. Is it a vengeful spirit attempting to rid itself of the living. Or is it a demonic spirit determined to destroy the souls of those they choose to harass? Or is it something else altogether? In 1948, in the small farming community of Macomb, one family found themselves faced with these very same questions.

In 1948, 13-year-old Wanet McNeill found herself in a situation she despised. For the last few years, Wanet's parents had been locked in a bitter divorce that tore the family apart. When the divorce was finalized, Wanet and her 8-year-old brother were sent to live with their father at her uncle's farm, the Willey Farm. Shortly after arriving at her new home small fires began popping up around the farm. Wanet was first thought to be the culprit as she took every opportunity to voice her displeasure with living on the farm. Although they were correct in suspecting her, they just couldn't understand how she was doing it.

The fires began as smoldering brown spots that suddenly burst into flames on the walls. When the fires became a day to day occurrence, the residents of the farm kept buckets of water around the house to douse the flames. The neighbors and the local fire department got involved to watch the mysterious fires. And to everyone's utter amazement the fires spontaneously erupted even if the main suspect wasn't present.

As the days passed the fires began to present a real threat to the house as well as the family. The Macomb Fire Chief became involved and opened up an investigation to the impossible fires. After carefully considering what to do, the Chief concluded that the best way to prevent the flames was to strip the walls bare of the wallpaper. Almost immediately several smoldering brown spots appeared on the walls in front of the incredulous Fire Chief and a dozen other eyewitnesses. The fire chief, at a complete loss of how this was happening, said,

"The whole thing is so fantastic, I'm ashamed to talk about it. We have a dozen witnesses that say they saw the brown spots appear and burst into flames." The fires and the investigation into the mysterious circumstances were beginning to heat up.

The week of August 7, 1948, saw the fires move from the bedroom walls to other areas of the house. Several people watched as the front porch burst into flames as well as the living room curtains and a bed was inexplicably engulfed in intensely bright flames. That week, the National Fire Underwriter's Laboratory became involved and made a few shocking discoveries. According to their investigation, the wallpaper where the fires initially started had been coated with a flame retardant flour-based paste. Upon further investigation, the NFUL discovered that no accelerant, such as gas or bug spray had been used to start the fires. This crack team of fire investigators could find no reason for these fires. It was as if the bowels of hell had burst forth and started the fires that threatened to destroy this family and their home.

The week following the investigation of the NFUL, the fires finally claimed the old farmhouse. The family watched in shock and despair as their beloved home burned quickly to the ground leaving nothing but a few smoldering embers. Wanet moved into the garage with her father and her brother, and that too, along with the milk house, erupted into a raging inferno. Upon hearing of the fires, the United States Air Force got involved. The flyboys theorized that the fires may have been caused by a secret Soviet directed radiation weapon. Even during the early days of Cold War paranoia, the eyewitnesses thought this theory was completely ridiculous. They questioned the Air Force investigators why the Reds would bother to target a farmhouse in rural Illinois. Following the protestations of the eyewitnesses, The Air Force bowed out saying nothing further on the subject.

On August 30, 1948, the authorities made a shocking announcement concerning the mysterious fires that destroyed the Willey farm. The fire marshal and the county sheriff announced that after hours of intense questioning, Wanet confessed to the fires. According to her confession, she was able to start the fires with nothing more than kitchen matches when no one was looking. As ridiculous as her confession sounded, the authorities insisted she started the fires because she didn't want to live on a dirty farm with her father. She wanted to live with her mother in the city and wear pretty dresses. According to them, the young girl was so distraught she decided to burn the whole thing down in a petulant temper tantrum to end all temper tantrums.

After the confession was made public, the people who witnessed the fires could not believe what they were hearing. Even the local newspapers were dubious on the girl's confession. A Peoria, Illinois newspaper that covered the bizarre events accused the authorities of using heavy-handed tactics to obtain a confession from the girl. And of course, they flatly denied the allegations.

To this day the fires that destroyed the Willey farm in Macomb are still considered one of the greatest mysteries in the land of Lincoln. No one involved believed that young Wanet McNeill was physically responsible for starting the fires that caused so much heartache. Researchers of psychic phenomena believe that Wanet was an unwitting focus of recurrent spontaneous psychokinesis due to the acrimony she held against her parents. It so, the case of the Macomb Poltergeist, should be considered the most destructive poltergeist of all time.

# Chapter 10: The Seven Gates Of Hell

The small southern Illinois town of Collinsville is a place that has long been associated with the mysterious. Situated on the outskirts of town is the Cahokia Mounds, a breathtaking pre-Columbian Native American city. A thousand years ago the Mississippian people built the mounds and the city that boasted a population of over 20,000 people. This once bustling metropolis is considered by archaeologists and paleontologists to be the biggest pre-Columbian city east of the Mississippi. And only a few years after being built, the people who lived and worked there mysteriously vanished.

Over the years several theories of why the citizens of this once-thriving city abandoned it has been offered by various experts. Some believe an outbreak of plague may have caused people to abruptly leave. Others think that war and famine may have decimated the population. While the more, shall we say, fringe researchers, believe that aliens simply took the people home. The mystery of why the citizens of Cahokia abruptly left their city does deserve further exploration. However, there is a ghostly mystery in Collinsville that both excites and terrifies the local teenagers and thrill-seekers alike, a mystery far more sinister than any ancient city.

Situated along Lebanon Road, just east of Collinsville is a series of tunnels the locals have dubbed 'The Seven Gates Of Hell.' According to the legend, if you drive through all the gates and pass through the seventh at the stroke of midnight, you and your car will find yourself in the pit of hell. Another variation states that if you stop your car in the seventh tunnel at midnight, Satan will send his hounds of hell to drag you screaming into his infernal domain. Of course, this begs the question – why?

Researchers of the strange and unusual really can't say with any degree of certainty how these seemingly innocent-looking tunnels received such a sinister reputation. One of the most enduring explanations may have arisen from the town's involvement with the infamous Ku Klux Klan in the 1950s and the activities of these criminals on the bridges.

According to the locals, it's believed that the KKK members used the bridges to lynch and hang young African American men. Although no records have ever surfaced to support this theory, locals are certain such atrocities occurred there long ago. People foolhardy enough to tempt the legend have reported seeing the ghostly bodies of young men hanging from the bridges as well as witnessing disturbing apparitions of those who met their fates at the hands of these cruel men.

The second commonly accepted theory of how these tunnels acquired their reputation concerns an automobile accident at one of the tunnels, a tunnel they call 'the acid bridge.' According to this unverified story, a group of teenagers were out for a fast paced joy ride while taking the hallucinogen, LSD. After passing through six of the gates they finally found the seventh, and it was just about midnight. With midnight quickly approaching, the driver, high on LSD, revved his engine, aimed his car, and hit the gas. Perhaps it was the drugs or it was too dark that night, but instead of passing through the gate, the car collided with the bridge instead. All of the hellbent teens were instantly killed when the car burst into flames incinerating their bodies. When people visit the acid bridge, they have reported seeing a ghostly car crashing into the side of the tunnel before bursting into a metal encrusted inferno. As the car vanishes the air is said to be filled with a deep sinister laugh.

An issue many researchers of the paranormal face is separating fact from those seemingly true sounding stories called urban legends. And the so-called Seven Gates Of Hell appears to be just that, an urban legend. Nevertheless, generations of Collinsville citizens insist the stories are true. Whether or not there is any truth to the stories of people going to hell after driving through these tunnels is highly unlikely. It's not something I am willing to find out.

# Chapter 11: The Spring Valley Vampire

In 1931, Director Tod Browning released his masterpiece of horror, *Dracula*, starring the great Bela Lugosi as the immortal undead nobleman. Since then we have been sold on the notion that these creatures of the night are handsome aristocrats who reside in a gothic castle, on the mist-shrouded cliffs of a dark mountain in a remote eastern European country. When it comes to the real vampire of folklore nothing could be further from the truth. According to the ancient folklore of many cultures, vampires are reanimated corpses, stalking the night seeking blood or revenge. They are by no means attractive, in fact, quite the opposite. One of these real vampires of folklore is believed to call Old Lithuanian Cemetery in Spring Valley, Illinois home. And it is neither handsome nor aristocratic.

One late night in 1967, two teenagers broke into the old Massock family mausoleum. As they vandalized the interior by spray painting all the walls, one of the teens stole a skull from one of the Massock brothers. When they exited the mausoleum they were horrified to discover a nightmarish creature waiting for them. Standing in front of them was a tall, white-skinned man wearing all black and eyes that burned red.

When the teens fled in terror, the horrific creature gave chase hissing and growling as it followed hot on their heels. The creature broke off its pursuit when the two boys exited the cemetery gates into the waiting arms of the local police. The two were arrested and charged with vandalism and grave robbery. However, the police could tell the two boys were terrified. When they asked what scared them so much, they told the police of the vampiric creature that chased them out of the cemetery. The story of what the boys encountered that night quickly got around and the legend of the Spring Valley was born.

For years following the initial encounter, stories of the vampire in Old Lithuanian Cemetery were frequently reported. The vampire was seen on numerous occasions emerging from the Massock family mausoleum and lurking about the headstones. Those who were courageous enough to enter the cemetery claimed to find the broken bodies of animals littering the cemetery drained of their most vital fluid, blood. Several people from the town reported their pets missing, while others claimed to see a gaunt, black-garbed figure in the cemetery. When the police responded to the cemetery to investigate, they found nothing. No sign of the vampire could be found.

One night in 1980, a man who described himself as a hardened Vietnam veteran entered the cemetery with his friends. The brave veteran wanted to see if there was any proof to these stories of a vampire and if there was, he was determined to kill it. As the vet and his companions walked through the cemetery, they were startled when an imposing figure that seemed to radiate pure evil suddenly appeared. The brave vampire hunter pulled a gun from his pocket and unloaded the clip into the creature. When he realized the bullets did not affect the being, the veteran and his friends fled the cemetery in terror.

Not long after the veteran's failed vampire hunt, researchers from Chicago arrived in Spring Valley to investigate the bizarre claims. On their first visit during the day, they claimed after finding the Massock mausoleum, they shoved a piece of wood in a crack. When they did so a long, black wormlike creature shot out and wrapped itself around the wood then vanished. Later that night, they returned and poured holy water into the crack where the black worm came out. They waited to see if the holy water would have an effect and were shocked when a loud agonized groan issued from the tomb. The researchers left the cemetery in a hurry believing that something dangerous and demonic resided there.

Since that night well over thirty years ago, reports of the vampire have become sporadic. And although the Spring Valley Vampire is considered nothing more than an urban legend, very few people are unwilling to find out for themselves if an ancient evil truly calls Old Lithuanian Cemetery home.

# Chapter 12: The Gate

If you were a teenager and grew up among the farms and small communities of northern Illinois, you were well acquainted with the fact that there isn't much to do. However, if you possessed an adventurous streak and a desire to explore the unknown you and your friends might travel to the town of Libertyville in Lake County, to investigate one of our most enduring legends. A location tainted by madness and mayhem. If this was your idea of a good time, then The Gate beckoned you.

Should you decide to check out this northern Illinois hotspot, you may find yourself somewhat disappointed. In the late 1990s, Independence Grove, a forest preserve, was expanded and The Gate was eliminated. Nevertheless, between the 1960s and the early 1990s, thrillseekers traveled the two miles down the fog-enshrouded River Road searching for the eerie Gate, a wrought iron fence between two white concrete structures. This may seem like some spooky innocent fun on a Saturday night, but what could have happened here that gave this rather unassuming gate it's frightening reputation? A reputation that has tempted local teens for decades may be down to a murder that may or may not have happened and a community's efforts to cover it up.

According to locals, there are two versions of the legend concerning The Gate and its dubious history. The first version claims that in the 1950s, The Gate was the entrance to an exclusive finishing school for the daughters of Chicago's wealthy elite. Its tranquil setting was perfect for young women to learn the manners and etiquette that was so very important to their parents and the social circles they were involved in.

That tranquility was devastated when the headmaster, for whatever reason, suffered a nervous breakdown. It is believed that on that night he stalked the halls of his school raving like a person who lost all connection with objective reality. When four of the students ventured into the hall to see what the commotion was. When the headmaster realized he had an audience, he murdered the four girls and hung their decapitated heads on the gate.

Of course, this story is undeniably grisly, nevertheless, it could be possible. Girls and young women from wealthy families did attend finishing schools that were located in the suburbs of Chicago. And there were always stories of inappropriate contact between staff and students. But, murderous rampages? I hardly think so. If this version of The Gate's history has some real-world possibility, the second version sounds like it was ripped from a 1980s slasher flick.

According to the second story, the gate was the entrance to a maximum-security asylum for the criminally insane. On a hot, dark summer night one of the patients, a bloodthirsty murderer, managed to escape his cell. As the asylum guards and police desperately searched the woods for the madman, the patient found his way to a nearby summer camp. The children slept peacefully in their cabin not knowing a dangerous lunatic lurked outside their cabin.

According to the story, the lunatic burst into the cabin and dragged four of the screaming children from their beds and slaughtered them. When the authorities finally caught up with him, they discovered to their horror that he came back to The Gate and mounted the heads of the children on it. Needless to say, the brute was gunned down by a sheriff's deputy. It was too little, too late.

Both of these stories are no doubt horrific in every detail. However, some researchers do believe that mass murder was committed at the location and the heads of the victims were mounted on the gate. You may ask, how did something so utterly horrific happen there and not gain national attention? Surely some record or report exists to back up these claims. It is believed that the town of Libertyville, to maintain its innocence and integrity, simply covered it all up and forgot about it. Whether or not murders happened there and if there was a conspiracy of silence, many visitors have reported some very intense encounters with the supernatural.

One of the most commonly reported paranormal experiences at the gate is said to happen on the anniversary of the murders. Visitors have reported seeing the heads of the four victims hanging from the gates as a bloodcurdling scream and blood issues from their mouths. Others have reported the apparitions of the children playing and laughing in the woods. Several people claimed to see the criminally insane murderer guarding the gate.

The Gate was knocked down almost twenty years ago by the Lake County forest preserve. Nevertheless, people claim to still have unexplained encounters where the dreaded Gate once stood.

# Chapter 13: Goon Road

In the towns of Girvan and Ballantrae in 16th century Scotland, the people found themselves faced with a disturbing mystery. Over the previous few years, a number of their fellow citizens had gone in the surrounding woods and hills to hunt and never returned. Several attempts to find their friends and family were made but never turned any solid leads. It was as if they just fell off the face of the Earth.

One day, while the townspeople were out searching for the latest disappearances near the coastal caves of Bennane Head, the searchers made a horrific discovery. Living in the caves was the 48 member family of Sawney Bean. It was further discovered the inbred Bean clan were cannibals as several dismembered bodies were stacked up in the caves as well as body parts of their victims were pickled. The clan of inbred man-eaters was arrested, and by order of King James VI, the Bean clan was executed in Glasgow. The horror of the Sawney Bean family was over.

The story of Sawney Bean and his clan of cannibals is considered by many historians as being nothing more than a grisly myth. Nevertheless, the story persists and may even have an American counterpart right here in the backwoods of Illinois, on a road known to the locals as Goon Road. If you're driving on Interstate 64, near the town of Fairview Heights, you will pass over a bridge on Bunkum Road. This road is usually avoided by the locals not because it's too treacherous to traverse but because it's believed the road is haunted and the surrounding woods are believed to be inhabited by the degenerate family of dangerous, inbred goons.

Many years ago, this family of goons lived in a ramshackle old house with a yard that looked like a junkyard. During the daylight hours, the goons slept, but at night this family of inbred goons left their house to hunt. Their game of choice wasn't deer or some other woodland creature, but rather humans. According to legend, the goons would jump out in front of cars driving along Bunkum Road. When the driver stopped, the goons would grab the unfortunate occupants and drag them into the woods kicking and screaming. After slaughtering their victims, the goons would take the corpses back to their house and chop them up for meals. Whatever scraps were left were thrown to their pack of wild dogs.

Today, the goons are gone, assuming the goons even existed at all. No records could ever be found to prove or disprove, their existence. However, this has not stopped thrillseekers from trying to find this family of murderous goons. A popular pastime for local teens is to stop their car at the bridge and yell into the woods, "Are you there goons?" Those courageous enough to test the legend have reported large lumbering shadows approaching them from the woods. Others have reported encountering packs of hell hounds roaming the woods after dark. A few people have even reported being physically assaulted by one of these large dark shadows, which are believed to be the ghosts of the goons.

If you should ever find yourself traveling on Interstate 64 late at night, don't stop on the bridge over Bunkum Road. You may just find yourself face to face with these monstrous goons or their pack of wild hellhounds.

# Chapter 14: The Chesterville Witch

In 1692, fear of the unknown gripped the small New England settlement of Salem, Massachusetts. This mass hysteria was kicked off when several young girls claimed the devil was afoot in their town and the heinous crime of witchcraft was being practiced by their fellow townspeople. When the accused were brought forward in the courtroom the girls would howl and scream as they writhed on the floor claiming to be bewitched. Not quite a year after the first accusations were made, 19 people tragically lost their lives and several more were imprisoned. False allegations of kissing the devil's behind and being in league with Lucifer were made and all these innocent people paid the price. This torrid episode is known today as the Salem Witch Trials and is still considered to be a black stain on the early history of the United States of America.

Allegations of witchcraft and devil worship are common throughout the history of western Christendom. In Scotland, England, and Germany thousands of innocent women lost their lives at the pointing of a finger and an accuser uttering the word, 'Witch.' Although the Salem witch trials are considered by historians to be the end of the hysteria, there were still small pockets of witchcraft accusations. One of those small pockets happened right here in Illinois.

Near the town of Arcola in central Illinois, sits the old town of Chesterville. Although it may not be on the map anymore, it was at one time a town populated mostly by the Amish. It is here that you will find a disused graveyard and a curious grave marker that simply reads, "A witch's grave." Not really something that you would expect to find in a graveyard in Illinois. As you stand and gaze at the grave marker and the tree that grows over the grave, you may find yourself asking, who was this woman? And why was she branded a witch?

In the Amish faith and other austere belief systems, the role women in these communities were sadly oppressed. The only functions women had were silent homemakers that gave their husbands sons. If women in Amish communities did anything more than that, they were dealt with harshly. And this is what brought about the fate of the woman that occupied the grave.

The so-called witch's name has been lost to time. Nevertheless, we know that she was a progressively minded person who spoke out against the mistreatment of women in the close-knit religious community. According to local historians, she was known to disrupt church services by debating biblical law with the elders and she refused to marry. This kind of behavior was so unacceptable the elders proclaimed she was in league with Lucifer and a practitioner of witchcraft. Without even so much as a trial, she was shunned and banished from the congregation, as well as the town.

Following the unfair sentence, the accused woman vanished without a trace. The community barely noticed as she was banished from the community. What did they care if she was gone? Being shunned is the same thing as having never existed at all. As far as they were concerned it was good riddance. A few days following her disappearance, her badly bruised and bloodied corpse was discovered in a cornfield not far from town. Despite the condition of her remains, which looked like she had been beaten to death, the elders concluded that the cause of death was natural causes.

The following day her body was taken to a local funeral home and the majority of Chesterville residents came to view the witch's body. With the viewing complete, the elders took the body to the Chesterville cemetery and gave her a proper Christian burial. However, the elders feared her spirit may return from the grave and exact vengeance on the town for the heinous miscarriage of justice she was subjected to. So, to keep her in her grave, they planted a tree over her body. When the burial was complete, the townspeople returned to their lives completely forgetting about the witch's grave.

Since that time, many years ago, there have been numerous reports of people encountering the spirit of the witch. The apparition of a grotesque old woman has been seen standing near the grave sometimes hiding behind the tree. Others have reported hearing cackling laughter issuing from the grave. One jogger reported, as he ran past the graveyard, an elderly woman beckoned him to join her by the grave. It is believed that if the tree is ever removed or if it dies, the witch's spirit will be unleashed upon the world to wreak vengeance on the town and its residents.

The witch's grave in the Chesterville graveyard is considered a curiosity by some. And to others, it is something to be feared. It is possible that this is just another falsely accused person in a long line of falsely accused people.

# Chapter 15: Graveyard X

Over the last decade, a new theory has surfaced that might just explain how spirit entities gain entrance to our material world. These doorways, or portals, are believed to be openings between our world and the spirit world that can be opened in two possible ways. The first of course being naturally occurring portals. These portals are said to exist on holy or sacred ground. The second kind of portal is believed to be intentionally opened through occult or magical means to communicate with the dead. Regardless of how portals are opened, they're not good as anything could come through. One of these naturally occurring portals appears to be in a small, rural graveyard in Illinois and its whereabouts is only known to a handful of people, a graveyard called Graveyard X.

When researching the background of Graveyard X, there really is nothing in its history that led it to be haunted. Before 1867, the land the graveyard sits on was owned by a farmer and was part of a cornfield. No major battles were fought here. No Native American burial grounds. Nothing tragic had ever occurred there that might contribute to the bizarre hauntings believed to happen there. The only thing that could remotely cause a haunting there was the lonely internment of a child in the 1870s

Since that time numerous encounters with the supernatural have been reported in this very nondescript rural graveyard. Dozens of unexplained photographs showing wispy apparitions have been captured in the cemetery. Those who know the whereabouts of this intensely haunted cemetery have even reported what could only be described as the feeling someone gets if a spirit passes through them leaving them with the eerie sense of familiarity with the spirit.

One of the most commonly reported phenomena in Graveyard X is the mysterious and unmistakable sound of children laughing and playing. No rational explanation has ever been ascertained, as Graveyard X is far away from any homes or schools and no children are present with the investigators.

The location of Graveyard X is a closely guarded secret, known to only a handful of researchers and investigators. And to be honest, it's probably best to keep it that way. It's feared that if the location of this graveyard was ever discovered, it would be opened up to the vandalism that plagues other haunted graveyards. If you should ever be lucky to learn the location of Graveyard X, you may want to consider keeping that knowledge to yourself.

# Chapter 16: Ashmore Estates.

In the field of paranormal research and investigation, it is commonly accepted that places, where tragedy occurs, are some of the most haunted locations in the world. Mental health facilities are one of those places that appear to have their fair share of hauntings. Psychiatric hospitals tend to be places of high emotion, unfinished business, and sadly, unexpected death. And Ashmore Estates is one of those psychiatric hospitals with a reputation of being extraordinarily haunted.

Founded in Ashmore, Illinois in 1915 as the Coles County Poor Farm, Ashmore Estates just seemed to be one of those places destined for hard times. The poor farm stayed in operation till the mid-1950s, when it closed its doors and reopened as s hospital for the criminally insane. In 1964, after experiencing financial difficulties and accusations of staff abuse, it closed down. In 2006 the building was reopened as a Halloween attraction. Although the new owners wanted to use this like a haunted house primarily for entertainment, they soon learned the building had its own real ghosts.

Patrons and haunted house employees reported witnessing large black masses moving down the halls and dodging in and out of rooms. Strange as it may seem, it almost appeared as if these black masses were looking for something in the rooms. These entities aren't as innocent as they may seem. There have been several reports of these entities chasing people around the building and shoving people to the floor before vanishing.

These black masses may be the most terrifying spirits at Ashmore Estates, but they are by no means the most active. The apparition of a little girl, Elva Skinner is the most active and encountered spirit at the former psychiatric hospital. In life, Elva Skinner was a little girl who lived there when it was the poor farm. According to historians, Elva perished in a fire that she may have inadvertently started by playing with matches. Elva is often experienced by playing innocent pranks on visitors. She has also been seen running through the halls laughing.

When it was discovered that Ashmore Estates was a haunted location, it became a popular destination for ghost hunters from all across the United States. It still operates as a Halloween attraction and if you're fortunate, you may just experience a ghost that isn't an actor in a sheet.

# Chapter 17: Willow Creek Farm

As a paranormal investigator, I specialize in an area where most investigators don't, private residences. Whenever I talk about my investigations in people's homes, I am inevitably asked what is the most haunted house I've ever investigated. Without even thinking about it my answer is a farmhouse located in the rural Illinois town of Shannon, at Willow Creek Farm.

In the 19th century, Illinois was still considered a frontier state on the edge of a young nation. Inhabitants of the East coast made their way to the Prairie state because they heard that purchase of the land was cheap and the soil was great for farming. However, things were not as simple or safe, as they were led to believe. In 1832, Apple Valley Fort was attacked by the Sauk and Fox tribes. Many settlers and Native Americans died during the conflict. The battlefield is still considered to be one of the most haunted locations in Illinois.

A few years after the grisly battle, William and Mary Boardman immigrated to the United States in 1835. They believed that Shannon was the place where all their dreams would come true. Without delay, they built a farm and started a family in their adopted country. The farm that would one day be Willow Creek Farm stayed in the Boardman family until as late as the 1980s. Unfortunately, financial problems caused the family to sell their ancestral home. The 21st century proved to be a turning point when in 2006, the old farm and land were purchased by Mr. Kilchner. Mr. Kilchner desired the peace he knew he would find on his new farm. What he didn't know was not only did he buy a farm, but bought the many ghosts that go with it.

Shortly after moving in, Kilchner began experiencing some very unexpected activity in his new home. Footsteps were heard throughout the house when he was the only person present. Inexplicable bangs and knocks were a common occurrence as were the bizarre sound of something rolling around on the second floor. And to add to the strangeness, the sound of children crying has been heard by the owner and his friends. The sound of Native American drums has also been heard on the land and in the house. If Mr. Kilchner was expecting peace and quiet, this old farmhouse may not be the place to find it after all.

The spirit activity may sound benign to most, nevertheless, much more aggressive spirit activity has been reported at Willow Creek Farm. Several visitors to the farm have reported the unpleasant feeling of fingers on their throats as if some unseen person was attempting to choke them. Apparitions and the bizarre entities known as shadow people have also been encountered by unsuspecting visitors. It is believed that between seven and nine spirits call Willow Creek Farm home and each one has been encountered.

One of the most often seen spirits is Sarah, a beautiful young woman wearing a floral print dress. Sarah has been seen throughout the house with a smile on her face. The second most commonly experienced spirit is an African American man named, Joe. This spirit is primarily encountered in the basement and it's believed he was an escaped slave making his way to freedom. Out of all the spirits believed to call this farm home, none is more terrifying than a disturbing spirit ominously dubbed, "The Creeper."

It is believed that in life, The Creeper was a medical doctor, Archibald Gram. When Dr. Gram was alive, he was known to fly into violent rages and subject his wife and children to horrific abuse. The spirit of Gram has been known to be aggressive to female visitors. Numerous women have accused this spirit of pushing, scratching, and hitting them. Gram reportedly resides in one of the second-floor bedrooms where he holds the spirit of a young boy named Robbie captive. Archibald Gram, MD was horrible in life and by all appearances, death has not changed that.

One might ask Mr. Kilchner chooses to reside in a home with nine spirits. To put it simply, Mr. Kilchner doesn't fear them and believes he and his spectral roommates can peacefully co-exist. Since discovering his house was haunted, Mr. Kilchner has allowed paranormal groups to investigate the spirits in his home. There is one stipulation he insists upon, be respectful. I can respect that, after all, he's the one that has to live with them.

In 2013, I was invited by a local paranormal group to join them for an investigation of Willow Creek Farm. Not much stood out concerning the reported paranormal activity. However, the end of the investigation would change that. As we sat at the table chatting, our attention was drawn to the basement door. It sounded as if someone was trying to open it. We watched in awe as the door inexplicably flew open. Of course, we investigated and found no reason how this could have happened. Perhaps it was just Joe saying hello.

# Chapter 18: The Great Kangaroo "Scare" Of 1974.

The year of 1974, proved to be an interesting year for world events. Richard Nixon became the first American president forced to resign due to the Watergate scandal. The hard rock band KISS hit the stage with their first album and changed the face of rock music forever. Muhammad Ali went 8 rounds with George Foreman and reclaimed the title of World Heavyweight Champion, proving to the world once again that he was the greatest. Although these and other great historical events took place in 1974, nothing came close to touching the weirdness that happened right here in Northern Illinois. In the remaining months of 1974, the citizens of the Chicagoland area encountered a beast that did not belong here.

In the early morning hours of October 18, 1974, Chicago police officers Leonard Ciagi and Michael Byrne were on patrol on the city's northwest side. For the most part, their shift had been a boring one with not much going on. At around 4 AM, their dispatch radioed them about a call they would have never expected. According to the dispatcher, they just received a call from a man who claimed that a kangaroo was standing on his front stoop. When they heard kangaroo the veteran police officers had a bit of a laugh. Nevertheless, it was a call, and despite the absurdity of it, it was something to break up the monotony of the shift.

When Ciagi and Byrne approached the house they were called to, their attention was drawn to the alley beside the house, and their humor was replaced by shock. Cornered against a wall stood a five-foot-tall animal that was most certainly a kangaroo. Confused as to what action to take, the two cops and the mysterious marsupial just stared each other down for a minute. When they regained their sense, the officers approached the out of place animal. Something they immediately regretted.

Officer Byrne took a few steps towards the animal that was now hissing and growling. Byrne took his handcuffs out and tried to cuff the kangaroo and out of fear and desperation, the animal attacked. The kangaroo landed several punches to the cop's face and kicked him in the shins. The patrolmen stunned and injured retreated and watched as the screeching kangaroo jumped over the fence and disappeared from sight. Their shift may have been boring, but now the veteran cops had one hell of a story to tell.

Following the initial encounter with the marsupial, several more were reported around the Chicagoland area. The next morning, in the suburbs of Oak Park a kangaroo was seen hopping through the neighborhoods. A newspaper delivery boy, as he was doing his route, reported that he watched as the kangaroo was almost hit by a car. Even the local police became involved when they received several calls from residents who reported a kangaroo was going through their trash.

As the reports of kangaroos were being made, it appeared that there was more than one kangaroo on the loose. In Plano, a town in Kendall County, several residents reported in shocked disbelief a kangaroo hopping through their backyards. The last known sighting of the mystery marsupial happened when a police officer saw one hunched over roadkill on South New England Avenue in Chicago. After that, the kangaroos just seemed to vanish.

When looking back at this bizarre episode of kangaroos in Chicago, you may find yourself questioning, how did these kangaroos get here from their native Australia. Of course, it was theorized that the animals were more than likely escapees from either a zoo or a circus. When these options were explored owners of zoos and circuses investigated and found that all their kangaroos were accounted for.

One of the more outlandish theories on how the kangaroos came to be in Illinois concerns the possibility that either they were transported here through wormholes. Or, for whatever reason, aliens picked up a few roos in the Australian outback and dropped them here in the prairies of the American Midwest. Yeah, I know, it sounds absurd but it's not as if there are herds of kangaroos hopping around Illinois. Or is there?

# Chapter 19: The Monster Of Stump Pond

Throughout the 1800s a lake monster was believed to make the choppy waters of Lake Michigan home. The creature was witnessed by hundreds of people who lived near the shores of Illinois's largest lake. Fisherman described the monster as being the size of a whale and serpent-like. The creature caused many to never step foot in the lake until it was captured or dead. And sometime around 1900, they got their wish. Whatever the monster was it suddenly vanished, never to be seen again.

Since before gaining statehood, there have have been numerous tales of monsters haunting the waters of the many lakes in Illinois. The Native tribes warned settlers to not swim or fish in certain lakes and rivers, because they may never return. Although these stories have been around for centuries, only two monsters in Illinois lakes have had more than just stories and a handful of eyewitnesses. Lake Michigan being one. The second, the monster of Stump Pond in downstate Du Quoin.

Reports of a monster in Stump Pond, which is actually a lake, started around the same time as the reports of the monster in Lake Michigan. The first sighting occurred in 1879 when a local fisherman was sitting in his point preparing to cast his line in the water. He was suddenly startled when a giant, snake-like fish rushed up to his boat and violently rocked his boat almost tossing him in the water. When he returned to town and told his tale of the beast, he described as being more than 10 feet long, and mean as hell. He had been fishing that lake since he was a child, but know more. Whatever the creature was caused this lifelong fisherman to never fish again.

The following Summer, several other fishermen encountered the monster of Stump Pond and their sighting was similar to that of the previous witness. The fishermen got a good look at the monster and described it as being twelve feet long, a dark green scaly body as thick as a telephone pole. They further said that it moved with the power of an alligator and the agility of a serpent. They watched it for several minutes before it sank beneath the water disappearing from sight.

If only a few people witnessed this creature it could be easily dismissed as nothing more than a fisherman's tale. The one that got away. But, for several years a creature matching the previous descriptions was seen by dozens of people. Including prominent citizens of Du Quoin and the surrounding area.

In the 1950s, Herb Heath, a respected businessman stumbled upon the creature while wading in Stump Pond. According to Heath, he startled the monster as it slept near the shore under a patch of moss. He watched as the creature quickly darted into the water. When Heath reported his sighting, he said the creature looked almost like an alligator and was taller than his 6-foot, 5-inch frame.

For the better part of the century residents of Du Quoin, Illinois were terrified to swim or fish in their lake. They feared something monstrous and potentially dangerous lurked in the lake. That was until 1968 when the town partially drained the lake. The only thing close to being considered monstrous were several larger than normal catfish. This revelation leads many to believe that the dreaded monster was nothing more than a large, overly aggressive catfish.

Most monster sightings can be dismissed as nothing more than misidentified animals, which is something that happens quite a bit in cryptozoology. However, we have dozens of eyewitness reports that would refute that conclusion. A large number of people familiar with the lake, and it's wildlife, believe they witnessed something strange that was most certainly not an overly aggressive catfish. It's a shame we will never know as the creature hasn't been seen in over 50 years.

# Chapter 20: The Ghosts Of Flight 191

Chicago's O'Hare International airport has been long considered one of the busiest airports in the world. With hundreds of national and international flights arriving and departing daily, it's an important port of call for the United States. I, myself have flown out of O'Hare several times and can think of no better airport to use. And although O'Hare is safe and free of a serious incident, this has not always the case. It was here in 1979, that one of the worst plane crashes in the history of aviation occurred. And many of the souls that perished in the crash still walk the scene where they died. May 25, 1979, was one of the busiest days in the history of the airport. It was Memorial Day, the official start of summer, and thousands were either departing or arriving for the long holiday weekend. At 3 PM, Flight 191 headed for Los Angeles, California was given clearance by the tower to take off. Shortly thereafter, the business of the airport was interrupted by a horrific event.

All appeared to go smoothly as Flight 191 left the tarmac and gained altitude. As the plane approached 300 feet, the tower controller became aware of something troubling. Parts of the port engine pylon began to fall off and a white vapor began shooting out of the engine. The tower then watched in horror as the engine itself fell off the plane. In a blind panic, tower control tried contacting the plane but it was too late. Everyone on that day in the airport and the surrounding area, watched the plane rolled and crashed to Earth in a field just east of Touchy Avenue. When it hit the ground, the plane erupted in a huge explosion killing all 271 passengers and flight crew.

Within minutes the crash of Flight 191 was reported all over the country and all across the globe. The safety of the airport was immediately brought into question and friends and family of the victims demanded answers. Those answers came after the National Transportation Safety Board (NTSB) wrapped up their investigation. And those desperately sought after answers were not good.

According to the findings of the NTSB on why Flight 19 crashed did not bode well for O'Hare. The NTSB discovered that a stress fracture in the flange that held the engine on caused the crash of the aircraft. When asked how something like that could be missed, investigators answered that flawed maintenance methods on the highly serviceable DC-10 were the cause. With the mystery of what caused the crash solved, maintenance crews became more vigilant when servicing planes. It became the airport's mission that never again would a tragedy of this magnitude happen at O'Hare international airport. With that mystery out of the way, another presented itself following the crash. A mystery that neither the NTSB nor O'Hare could solve.

A few days after the crash the Des Plaines Police Department began receiving phone calls from people seeing something out of the ordinary in the field where the plane crashed. Strange white lights were witnessed bobbing among the grass. Believing that ghoulish souvenir hunters were trespassing, several officers were dispatched to investigate. If people were indeed trespassing in that field they could potentially face serious fines and be arrested. Unfortunately, when the police arrived and searched the field they found no trace of any trespassers. No sign of anyone that could cause the lights.

The lights in the field might seem mysterious enough. Nothing could match the level of strange activity being reported in the mobile home community adjacent to the airport. Residents of the community became that strange things were afoot when they would hear footsteps coming up the stairs to their front door and furious knocking on the door. When they opened the door to see who was there, they found nothing on the other side. Dogs seemed to be the ones most affected by the activity. For no reason, dogs would start barking at something only they could see.

Over the years residents of the mobile home park experienced much more than barking dogs and unexplained knocking. Several residents reported coming face to face with the apparitions knocking on their doors. When they opened the door they were shocked to see horribly injured men and women in tattered clothing either begging for help locating their luggage or talking about making their connecting flights. They then watched as the figures turned and vanished.

It has been over forty years since 271 people lost their lives when Flight 191 crashed in a giant ball of flames. Residents of the area still report unexplained footsteps and knocks on their doors at all hours of the day and night. Reports of encountering apparitions, although rare,

are still reported by residents. The activity has even caused several residents to sell their mobile homes. But when new residents move in they too experience similar frightening activity. The souls of the passengers of Flight 191 may never find the peace and rest they desire, forever forced to walk the grounds where their lives were abruptly stolen from them.

# Chapter 21: Top 5 UFO Sightings

Here in Illinois, there have been several encounters with the otherworldly craft that leads researchers in UFOlogy to believe the land of Lincoln is a window area. A window area is a location with an unusually high number of UFO sightings. These are the top 5 reported encounters with UFOs in Illinois.

*The Wayne City Chase*

On the night of August 4, 1963, a young couple was at a drive-in theater at 11:30 PM, when an event occurred that would forever change their perception of reality. As the young man drove down the country road, his attention was drawn to a bright white object silently flying just above the trees. He described the object as fuzzy, without form, and about the size of a bathtub. The couple briefly talked about the strangeness of the object but didn't consider it dangerous by any means.

When the young man began picking up speed, he noticed something that was somewhat disturbing, the bright light kept pace with his car. He further reported that when he took his foot off the gas pedal and slowed down the craft would slow down as well. Fear began to take hold and the young couple worried that something truly out of the ordinary was happening. Not wanting to find out if there was any truth to their suspicions, he picked up speed and didn't stop until he pulled up in front of his girlfriend's house.

When they ran into the house, the girl hurriedly switched off all the lights in the house. When they peeked out the window they were horrified to see that whatever this thing was remained and was hovering in the sky just outside her house. They both had the impression that something intelligent was guiding the craft and watching them. The young man remarked that what they were experiencing seemed like something straight out of a bad science fiction movie. If this was something not of this world, what we're it's intentions? And why on Earth did it choose to harass them?

After watching the hovering light for fifteen minutes, the young man decided to gather his courage and go home. He darted out of the house and jumped into his car peeling away as fast as he could. The frightened young man would later tell investigators that as he drove away from his girlfriend's house, the craft changed its color from brilliant white to a dull orange. According to the young man, the craft finally broke off its pursuit when he pulled into his driveway and ran into the house.

As far as we know there weren't any other sightings or reports of the light and its curious behavior. This fact has led many researchers to believe this was nothing more than a hoax. But for what purpose? The couple didn't report their encounter until many years later and the details of the craft and their insistence never wavered. This young couple clearly had an experience, but whether or not it was alien in origin is the only debatable issue.

### *The Franklin Park Encounter*

When parents sign their sons up for the Boy Scouts there are certain skills they expect them to learn. Good manners, loyalty, and responsibility to name a few. What parents don't expect is their children coming face to face with the otherworldly and unexplained. And that's exactly what a den of Boy Scouts got in the town of Franklin Park, a suburb on the northwest side of Chicago.

On May 28, 1979, a Boy Scout leader was leading his pack of thirteen boys on a hike up Blueberry Hill, a hike this leader had taken several times before, but today, the inexplicable occurred. As the leader and his pack approached the top of the hill, they were startled when a high pitched whine sounded from over their heads. The bizarre noise prompted them to search for the origin of the strange whine and when they looked up what they saw was something not of this world.

Hovering fifty to sixty feet above the ground was a pulsating, metallic saucer approximately twenty-five feet long with a highly reflective bottom that the Scouts could see themselves in. They further reported a reddish glow that emanated from the spinning dome and an eerie purplish mist surrounded the craft giving it an ethereal look.

After observing the craft for several seconds any fear that the leader and the scouts had was now replaced by curiosity. All thirteen boys and their leader knew instinctively that whatever this craft was, was not something built by man. As they observed the craft, the saucer let out another high pitched whine and began to move away and then shot into the sky at an impossible rate of speed. Within mere moments the saucer vanished from view. When the scouts and their leader reported the close encounter they all agreed the sighting only lasted thirty seconds. No other sightings of a flying saucer have been made at Blueberry Hill.

### *The Downers Grove Attempted Landing*

On a July evening in 000 at 8 PM a security guard in a Downers Grove office building was conducting routine rounds when his attention was drawn to something strange outside a window. When he got closer to the window, he was shocked to see several bright lights hovering over the south parking lot. Believing that a helicopter was attempting to land in the parking lot of the building he was paid to secure, he ran out to the parking lot fully prepared to tell the pilot to land somewhere else. He would soon discover this was no helicopter.

When he ran out into the south parking lot, he looked up to see a large, cigar-shaped object as long as eight school buses and just as high. He further described the craft as being silver/blue in color with a gold strip wrapped around it. The security guard later reported that whatever the craft was it hovered over the parking light and it appeared that it wanted to land.

Thankfully the security guard wasn't the only one to witness the unidentified flying object. Several tenants from a nearby apartment building and the building's cleaning crew joined the stupefied guard. The ever increasing crowd of onlookers watched in awe as the uncanny craft rose into the air and quietly moved off to the east.

### *The Urbana-Champaign Lights*

Since the late 19th century, the twin towns of Urbana and Champaign have been synonymous with higher education. In 1867, John Milton Gregory established the University of Illinois, a school that is considered to be one of the best liberal arts colleges in the prairie state. However, in the early years of the 21st century, the college town became the site of strange lights and close encounters with UFOs.

Shortly before midnight on February 2, 2002, several students at the university and residents of the twin towns reported something unexplained flying overhead. They beheld several clusters of red-hued lights silently flying southwest to the southeast. The majority of the eyewitnesses regarded the lights as nothing more than small airplanes out for a late-night flight. Nevertheless, one witness, a local police officer did not have the luxury to be quite so dismissive.

While on patrol the police officer had been hearing some of the strangest chatter he had ever heard on his radio. Several residents of the town and students reported witnessing unexplained lights and aircraft that could not possibly be of this world. Of course, the officer was skeptical, and understandably so, as to him, such things could not exist. All that disbelief came crashing down around him when he pulled into the parking lot of Memorial Stadium.

The patrolman watched as several objects hovered silently over the stadium. He was about to call the sighting into his dispatch when a bright light similar to a spotlight shot out from underneath the craft into the stadium. The police officer, in his remarks to his superiors, stated that it almost seemed as if the craft were searching for something. He then surveilled as the spotlights shut off and the craft abruptly vanished into thin air.

Since that frosty winter night in 2002, there have been no further reports of strange lights or unexplained craft in or around the college. Most have dismissed the sightings as either a hoax or an elaborate prank played for laughs by students. Nevertheless, we have the testimony of the police officer who went on record stating that what he saw was by no means a prank. When you consider the words of the police officer concerning the searchlights, you can't help but inquire, what were the craft looking for? For our sake, I hope they found it.

## The Rockford Lights

On the night of March 13, 1997, thousands of people in the city of Phoenix, Arizona and it's surrounding area, witnessed an awe-inspiring sight. For approximately 3 hours, 7:30 pm-10:30 PM, strange lights in a V-shaped formation appeared over the city. Leading up to this event there were several other reports of lights and a V-shaped craft flying soundlessly over the desert. This event has been called the Phoenix Lights by researchers and is considered the greatest mass sighting of UFOs in history. However, a mere three years later in Rockford, Illinois a mass sighting occurred that gave the Phoenix Lights a run for its money.

Since February 2000, hundreds of reports of large, yellow-colored orbs of light have been seen over the skies of the Northwest Illinois city. Some of these lights have even been reported flying in what some have described as, battle formation. Giving some the impression that perhaps these lights could potentially have malicious intent.

In January 2001, WREX Channel 13 aired a special segment on the lights being regularly seen flying over the city. According to the report, the local police logged over 600 reports of unexplained lights made by Rockford residents. And it wasn't just the yellow orbs people were witnessing. Several reports were of the large triangular-shaped craft seen flying in formation over the city were made. Keeping with your typical encounters with alleged alien aircraft, people also experienced electrical problems in their homes and cars. Fortunately, no one has ever reported being abducted by the crews of these alleged alien spacecraft. Well, not yet anyway.

These five close encounters with possible extraterrestrial craft are but a small sampling of the hundreds of reported sightings in Illinois since the beginning of the modern UFO era. The land of Lincoln does appear to be a window area where extraterrestrial and possibly interdimensional beings come and go at will. It really leaves you questioning, are the cornfields attracting them? Or, perhaps it's Chicago's happening nightlife. If I ever meet one I'll be sure to ask.

# Chapter 22: The Enfield Monster

Many people don't realize that among the cornfields and the concrete and steel of our many cities, Illinois has large forested areas that stretch on for hundreds of miles. It's in these forests of southern Illinois that many strange creatures and terrifying cryptids are said to live. In 1973, one of these nightmarish creatures emerged from the woods surrounding the sleepy town of Enfield in Southern Illinois. A creature so grotesque it caused a panic that is still talked about today.

The peculiar events began on the night of April 25, 1973, when lifelong Enfield resident, Henry McDaniel, came face to face with a beast ripped from nightmares. McDaniel had just returned home from a long day at work and all he wanted to do was crack open a beer and watch a little TV before falling into a much-needed sleep. A few moments after sitting down in his favorite easy chair, McDaniel became aware of a noise at his front door. To him, almost sounded like some animal was scratching at it. And considering all the stray cats and raccoons in the woods he wouldn't be surprised if that's what it was.

McDaniel tried to ignore the annoying sound, but when it didn't stop he angrily got up from his chair and threw open the door. He thought if it was a stray cat he could easily scare it off. But when he opened the door he was shocked to see a creature that could have only come from his worst nightmares. Standing on his front porch was a short gray-colored creature with two short arms protruding from its chest, two unusually large pink eyes and to top it off, three legs. When McDaniel regained his good sense, he slammed the door shut and stood with his back against the door. He didn't know what to do about the horrific creature standing on his porch. And then it came to him, the only thing he could think of to rid himself of the monster.

When McDaniel returned from his bedroom with his pistol he threw the door open, took aim at the hairy interloper's chest, and fired one round. McDaniel knew that he hit the monster, but it appeared unfazed. Whatever this thing was it let out a loud angry screech and jumped away, covering at least seventy-five feet with only three jumps. McDaniel watched as it disappeared into the woods.

Following the departure of the creature, McDaniel called the White County Sheriff's Department to report his encounter with the monster. Not long after his call, Sheriff Roy Poshard and an Illinois State patrolman responded to the frightened man's house. Poshard was already well acquainted with Henry McDaniel as he was a well known drunkard. But after talking with him for a few minutes the lawman could tell he wasn't drunk and perhaps he did something he couldn't wrap his mind around.

At first, Poshard couldn't believe what he was hearing. The creature McDaniel was going on about sounded like something out of a corny 1950s monster movie. He tried convincing McDaniel that he hadn't seen a monster until his deputy found something inexplicable. Leading into the woods were animal tracks, but not like any animal tracks they had ever seen. These tracks had six toe pads rather than five and they knew that wasn't possible. McDaniel was so excited by what he had seen he told Poshard that he intended to tell everyone. When the Sherrif heard that, he sternly warned McDaniel that if he did he would be signing his own arrest warrant. The last thing the Poshard needed was a panic in his County and fear of a monster would certainly do just that. McDaniel relented, but it wouldn't be the last time he saw the creature.

While the police searched McDaniel's property they didn't realize that the mystery animal was closer than they thought. Greg Garrett, an 8-year old-neighbor of McDaniel, was playing in his backyard when the monster attacked. Well sort of. Little Greg watched as the creature hopped over the fence into his yard and when he tried to play with it, the creature let out an ear-piercing screech. Greg tried to flee but the creature jumped on his feet and tore his brand new tennis shoes. The frightened boy retreated into his house and through his tears told his parents what he encountered. Greg's parents tried to calm their son, but to no avail, Greg had nightmares for weeks following the attack.

Two weeks later, the creature once again returned to Henry McDaniel's home. On May 6, McDaniel was awakened by the sound of howling and barking dogs. When he looked out the window, he saw the creature standing by the railroad tracks by his house. This time McDaniel didn't shoot at the creature but he did defy the orders of Poshard. The next day he told everyone in town that a possibly dangerous monster was lurking in the woods surrounding the small town. And just like Sheriff Poshard feared, a full-on panic set in, and every trigger happy good old boy wanted to bag themselves a beast.

Within days of McDaniel's report curiosity seekers, newspaper reporters and self-described monster hunters descended on the town like the biblical plague of locusts. Among the courageous monster hunters was a group of 5 rifle-toting young men who locked and loaded and ready to take down the bloodthirsty beast. But rather than shooting the creature, one of the guys shot one his buddies in the leg and all five were taken into custody and charged with disturbing the peace, discharging a firearm outside of hunting season, and the lesser charge of pissing the Sheriff of White County off.

Not all the monster hunters were necessarily a danger to themselves and society, one hunter rolled into town brandishing a microphone. Rick Rainbow, a news director from an Indiana radio station, came to Enfield with three friends to capture evidence of the beast. Rainbow did spot the beast near an abandoned house. But, the only evidence he managed to capture was a tape recording of the creature's plaintive cry.

Not long after Rainbow's visit, the sightings of the monster ended just as abruptly as they started. Since those weird spring nights in 1973, several theories have been offered to explain the creature. And as one would expect the explanations are just as fantastic as the beast. UFOlogists believe the creature may have been an alien that accidentally got left behind when his ship blasted off to the stars. Another theory was that it was a baby Bigfoot. And the third theory connects it with another mystery creature sighting that took place a year later. Some believe it may have been an escaped kangaroo. No one can really conclude as to what the Enfield Monster, but it has never returned to the town it, well, annoyed 45 years ago.

# Chapter 23: Thunderbirds

Before white European settlers came to the North American continent, the native tribes lived in peace and harmony with the natural world. Every rock and tree had a spirit and in many tribes, animals were more than pets or prey, they were considered part of the family. Living close to nature these people were intimately aware of every animal they shared their environment with. Even animals that we may consider to be monstrous and one of those monstrous creatures was the legendary Thunderbird.

According to Native American legend, the Thunderbird was a giant bird with a huge wingspan that would block out the sun as it glided overhead. The Thunderbird was considered to be both a friend and a potential enemy to man. On the friend side, the flapping of the thunderbird's wings brought the storms that the crops needed to grow. But, on the enemy side, these frightening birds of prey were known to silently dive out of the sky and carry away livestock and allegedly children and warriors. These predatory birds played an important part in the legends and lore of just about every Native tribe. But they couldn't have existed, right?

During the Pleistocene era, large predatory birds called teratorns ruled the skies of prehistoric North America. It's believed they became extinct sometime around the end of the last ice age 50,000 years ago. The largest of these birds the Teratornis Merriami was double the size of America's largest bird, the California condor. According to the fossil record, this formidable airborne predator would have been over 3 feet long from beak to tail feather and a wingspan close to twenty feet. Such an impressive avian terror could have easily carried away in its dagger-like talons a large dog and perhaps a child. When considering the epoch that these birds existed, it's quite possible early man would have dealt with this monstrosity swooping out of the sky carrying away pets and possibly children. Thankfully the teratorn went extinct tens of thousands of years ago. Or did it?

Stories of giant birds have persisted even into our modern era from all over the North American continent. But it is here, in the state of Illinois that these winged terrors might still call home. And two of these birds may have been responsible for the attempted abduction of an eleven-year-old boy in 1977.

Back in the late 1600s, Illinois was still a vast wilderness untouched by the European settlers that lived on the east coast. In 1673, Jesuit priest, Father Jacques Marquette, an early explorer of Illinois saw a fearsome sight. While sailing up the Mississippi River near Alton, the priest saw a painting on a limestone bluff that was the stuff of nightmares. Father Marquette, described this horrific beast as having the body as large as a calf with the horns of a goat. The creature's eyes burned red with fire and it had a beard like a tiger and the face of a man. When Marquette inquired as to who painted the beast, nobody knew. Nevertheless, according to the tribes in the area the Piasa, as it was called, was a beast like no other and greatly feared.

It would be simple to just dismiss this as another example of a legendary creature if it wasn't for the horrific find of a college professor in 1836. John Russell, a professor at Shurtleff College heard the legend of the Piasa and wanted to see if there was any truth to the legend. When he arrived in Illinois, he hired a Native American guide that could lead him to the possible lair of this ferocious creature.

After traveling up the Illinois River, Russell and his guide made an arduous climb up a cliff and came upon a cave in the rock face. When they entered the cave they discovered a disturbing sight. Covering the floor of the cavern were thousands of human and animal bones picked clean of flesh. Russell believed this charnel house could be the lair of the legendary Piasa bird. Russell's guide was so frightened by what they had seen he demanded to flee before whatever creature that lived here returned. John Russell was all too happy to oblige.

Modern researchers believe the painting of the ferocious Piasa bird may be a representation of the legendary Thunderbird. Although this giant bird appears in the fossil record, and the traditions of the native tribes, it's believed to be long since extinct. Nevertheless, according to some eyewitnesses, it is still very much alive and it has not lost its ferocity.

The most dramatic encounter with an alleged Thunderbird occurred in the small southern Illinois town of Lawndale in 1977. In July of that year, several people claimed to see two giant black birds ominously circling the town. Those that witnessed the birds described them as being jet black with a white ring around their necks. But it was the size of the birds that terrified the witnesses the most. According to them, the bird's bodies were the size of full-grown men and their wingspans easily exceeded twenty feet. Residents of the town were wise to keep their pets indoors as they feared these birds swooping out of the sky and making their dogs and cats a meal. The birds, however, had a much different prey in mind.

In the early evening hours of July 25, 10-year-old Marlon Lowe, and his friends were playing in the backyard of his parent's house when the unthinkable happened. As Marlon and his friends were chasing each other around and laughing when their attention was drawn to the sky upon hearing a loud screech. They watched in horror as a giant black bird swooped out of the sky, grabbed Marlon by his shirt, and lifted him off the ground. Marlon screamed and attempted to fight his avian attacker off, but it was far too strong for the gangly child. Thankfully his mother heard his cries and ran outside to rescue her little boy. After several minutes of hitting the bird, the bird released Marlon and flew away.

Following the attack, several neighbors who had witnessed the attack ran over to see if the boy was ok. Marlon suffered a few scratches and a horrific memory that would last him the rest of his life. When the police came to take the report of the attack, the witnesses, including Marlon described the bird as being jet black, with a ring of white around its neck. It was estimated the powerful bird lifted Marlon 3 feet off the ground and carried him 35 feet. Whatever this bird was it was not normal.

A few days following the attack of Marlon Lowe, a nearby farmer, his wife, and some friends spotted two large birds over his farm in McClean county. The farmer reported that he and the small party were watching radio controlled airplanes when a giant black bird flew up to the planes. The farmer claimed the wingspan of the bird easily dwarfed the RC planes. The farmer reported his sighting to the sheriff who considered him to be a credible witness.

The summer of 1977 turned out to be the summer for sightings of giant birds. So far no one had been able to capture any evidence of giant black birds terrifying the skies of southern Illinois. Finally at the end of the summer, Texas John Huffer a local Native American man managed to film the birds. As he was fishing, Huffer's attention was drawn to two giant black birds roosting in a tree. When the birds took the air, Huffer grabbed his camera and began filming the anomalous animals. Fearing the birds might attack, Huffer sounded his boat horn and scared the birds off. Huffer's film is still considered to be proof positive that Thunderbirds still exist.

Since that Summer in 1977, reports of giant black birds flying through the skies of Illinois has dramatically dropped off. A handful of reports have been made here in Illinois and other states, however, critics agree these may just be miscalculations of known predatory birds. Nevertheless, we have the attack of Marlon Lowe and several credible eyewitnesses who refute the critics. It's highly likely early Native Americans did deal with giant birds at one time, but according to mainstream science these birds died out millennia ago. Either people are dealing with a species of bird that is believed to be dead or something else entirely.

# Chapter 24: The Eastland Disaster

On the morning of April 15, 1912 people in the United States and across Europe awoke to terrible news. Over 1500 people lost their lives when the RMS Titanic hit an iceberg and sank to the bottom of the frigid waters of the North Atlantic ocean. The sinking of this supposedly unsinkable ship has gone down as being the greatest maritime tragedy in the history of the world. A few years later, in Chicago, Illinois the second worst maritime tragedy happened along the shores of the Chicago River.

On the morning of July 24, 1915, the Western Electric Company planned a picnic for its employees and their families as a thank you for their hard work and dedication. The company chartered four steamships to carry the 7000 people across Lake Michigan to Michigan City, Indiana for the festivities. The four ships were moored along the Clark and LaSalle Street bridges. Sadly, tragedy struck before they left the dock.

Since the beginning of sailing, it has been a tradition for passengers on a ship to gather on deck and bid farewell to those that could not join them. Historians believe that it was this tradition that may have caused this disaster on the Chicago River. According to the people who witnessed the tragedy hundreds of the Eastland gathered on deck waving goodbye. As the ship eased away from the dock it began to tilt dangerously. As the ship struggled to leave the dock, the Eastland capsized throwing passengers into the Chicago River and trapping hundreds of others under the water. The other three steamers desperately tried to save the passengers by throwing out lines and life preservers. Sadly, their courageous attempts failed as the wake of the capsized ship swamped the passengers drowning them.

When rescuers from the Chicago Fire Department arrived on the scene their eyes were met with a scene of complete chaos. Everyone present did what they could to rescue the victims. When all was said and done 835 passengers including 22 families lost their lives. When the disaster was investigated it was discovered the ballast compartments designed to give the ship stability were emptied to make room for passengers. It's believed this may have caused the ship to capsize, however, when the investigation was completed they were unsure what caused the Eastland to roll. Perhaps this explains why some of the souls of the victims refuse to rest.

When the bodies from the Eastland Disaster were recovered from the Chicago River, over 200 bodies were transported to the 2nd regiment armory for identification. Decades later in 1984, the building was converted into Harpo Studios where Oprah Winfrey's wildly successful day time talk show was filmed. Shortly after Oprah's show began people who worked in the building began reporting unexplained activity and even encounters with spirits believed to belong to those who perished on the Eastland.

Night security guards and people working late in the building have reported hearing invisible children running around the building and laughing. Disembodied voices and the sounds of footsteps on the stairs are heard at all hours of the night. As well as doors being opened and slammed by unseen hands. But it is the appearance of the apparition of a woman in a gray dress seen wandering the halls that have scared a few employees away. Oprah has never confirmed or denied the rumors that her studio was haunted but her employees had plenty of stories to tell. Winfrey may no longer do her show but the building is still considered to be one of the most haunted places in Chicago.

The hauntings at the former Harpo Studios is not the only place said to be haunted by the souls of the Eastland victims. According to numerous reports, the site of the disaster is said to be haunted as well. Near the Clark Street bridge, the sounds of screams and pleas for help have been heard coming from the water. A few visitors to the bridge have even reported seeing the apparitions of people wearing clothes from that era walking across the bridge.

Today, a plaque stands at the Clark Street bridge in remembrance of the disaster and its hundreds of victims. It is said that if you stand at the plaque and listen closely you may just hear the wails of those who tragically perished in the waters of the Chicago River over a century ago.

# Chapter 25: The House With Round Corners

If you were a teenager in the far northern suburbs of Illinois, chances are you were familiar with the tiny Town of Bull Valley. This small town in McHenry County was the stuff of Urban legends, and some respects, nightmares. According to the rumors that ran rampant throughout McHenry and Lake counties, Bull Valley was overrun with worshippers of the Prince Of Darkness.

Among the many dark tales concerning Bull Valley, the town had no Christian churches within city limits. The Satanists that controlled the city council refused to award any religious institution a permit to build any houses of worship in their town. Even the streets of Bull Valley are designed to take the shape of a pentagram if observed from the air. We all grew up hearing tales of sinister forces at work in Bull Valley.

As it goes with the majority of these stories, it's all completely false. There are plenty of churches in Bull Valley and the roads are not shaped like a pentagram. Nevertheless, in Bull Valley, there is a house that has earned itself the distinction of being the most haunted house in Illinois. The Stickney Mansion, or as it has been called for many years, the house of round corners.

In the mid-1800s, Illinois was still considered to be on the fringes of America. It was wild and quiet and very few people called the vast prairie lands home. It was these features that attracted George and Sylvia Stickney. George and Sylvia were devout adherents to the burgeoning religion of Spiritualism and Sylvia, by all accounts was a talented medium. The isolation of Bull Valley was perfect for communing with the spirit world. So, in 1856, George Stickney built a grand, two-story mansion where they could throw parties and seances for their friends and clients, a mansion with a very unique design.

When the house was being built, Sylvia insisted the entire second floor should be an elegant ballroom that boasted the first piano in northern Illinois. Neither the ballroom nor the piano was what gave the house it's unusual reputation. Both George and Sylvia believed that evil spirits could hide in 90-degree angles and avoid detection, a common belief among Spiritualists at that time. To avoid this happening, the Stickneys insisted that the house should have no corners. They insisted the walls be rounded for protection.

According to legend one corner of a room came to an unfortunate 90-degree angle. Perhaps the corner was by accident or the builder didn't share in the Stickney's religious convictions. No one really knows for certain how this happened, but this unfortunate corner took a turn for the worse.

The story goes that Sylvia returned from town and made a horrible discovery. Slumped over in the one corner was the lifeless body of the man of the house, George Stickney. Following an examination by a physician, it was determined George died from a massive heart attack. Sylvia, of course, believed otherwise. Sylvia believed that an evil spirit took up residence in the corner and murdered her beloved husband. One would think this tragic turn of events would cause Sylvia to flee the house that took the life of her husband. On the contrary, Sylvia Stickney remained in the house for many years following the death of George. Sylvia became a world-famous medium and continued throwing parties and seances for clients and friends until the day she herself passed into the Summer Lands.

Following the death of Sylvia Stickney, the house with round corners sat empty for many decades. Strangely enough, despite its voluminous history with the spirit realm, it was never considered to be haunted by the locals. The house was considered to be nothing more than an enigma silenced by its many years of being empty. All that would change in the 1970s, when a local man purchased the house and moved in.

In the mid-1970s, Rodrick Smith bought the house with round corners and resided in it for several years. It wouldn't be until he moved out that the unusual house would gain its reputation for being haunted. Smith reported that while living there he was bothered by strange activity at night. He claimed to hear the sounds of footsteps in the hall as well as music and voices on the second floor. Smith further reported that his dogs never felt comfortable in the house and would bark incessantly at things only they could see. Up to that point, Smith never believed in ghosts and would often scoff at the notion of an afterlife. His tune would soon change when he did some historical research and discovered disturbing details concerning his home.

According to Smith, he discovered that in the 1960s the house was used as a meeting place for a group of Satanists. These devil worshippers knew of the history of the house and felt it would be perfect to hold black magic rituals to raise the dead. Upon hearing of these rituals happening in Bull Valley, the residents were scandalized by such wickedness in their midst.

It was later discovered that Smith wasn't being honest about his findings. It turned out these so-called Satanists were nothing more than hippies who were squatting in the house when it was empty. The graffiti the hippies left on the walls and the drug paraphernalia they left behind was mistaken for trappings of the occult. Smith's story came crashing down around him and the house once again sat empty.

With the stories of black magic rituals being thoroughly debunked, this did not stop the ghost stories surrounding the mansion. A local antique dealer, while looking at an ad for the house discovered something otherwordly in a photo. In an ad for the house, the antique dealer claimed to see the image of a young woman in a wedding dress peering out a window. When he brought it to the attention of the real estate agent, the agent insisted that whoever this woman was, he did not see her when he snapped the photo.

Today, the house with round corners has a much different occupant. One that doesn't scare so easily, the Bull Valley Police Department. The police insist there is nothing to the stories of the mansion being haunted. However, a few former officers tell a much different story. When they worked there, it was common to hear footsteps and voices coming from the empty rooms in the house. A couple of officers claimed to have seen the young woman in the wedding dress out of the corner of their eyes. They're not sure who this white lady is, but they believe she is there.

The house with round corners or the Stickney Mansion presents a dilemma for researchers of psychic phenomena. It's one of those instances where you have to separate potentially real supernatural activity from urban legend. If the stories are to be believed, then this unusually constructed house may just be the most haunted house in Illinois. If not, then it just stands as a testament of just how weird the state of Illinois really is.

# Final thoughts

I love the state of Illinois and will forever consider it home. Whether you come here to delve into the criminal history of Chicago, our largest city. Or experience the weirdness the rest of the state has to offer you may just find yourself coming back again and again. Just keep in mind you're always welcome in one of the weirdest states in the United States of America. So, again I saw, welcome to Illinois. Come for the hospitality. Stay for the weirdness.

www.ingramcontent.com/pod-product-compliance
Lightning Source LLC
Chambersburg PA
CBHW031125250726
48655CB00002B/515